WHO TOOK MOLLY BISH?

A shocking true story of pursuit for justice in the
abduction and murder of 16-year-old Molly Bish

SARAH L. STEIN, PH.D.

FOREWORD BY

JOHN W. DRAWEC, ESQ.

DR. SARAH STEIN
WHEN CRIMINAL JUSTICE FAILS

DrSarahStein.com
#TheTinyAvenger

Who Took Molly Bish? – 1st ed.
Sarah L. Stein, Ph.D.

Cover Design by AlyBlue Media, LLC
Interior Design by AlyBlue Media LLC
Photos by Dr. Sarah L. Stein
Published by AlyBlue Media, LLC

ISBN: 978-1-950712-32-8
AlyBlue Media, LLC
Ferndale, WA 98248
www.AlyBlueMedia.com

This book is designed to provide informative narrations to readers. It is sold with the understanding that the author or publisher is not engaged to render any type of legal, psychological, or any other kind of professional advice. The content is the sole opinion and expression of the author. No warranties or guarantees are expressed or implied by the choice to include any of the content in this book. Neither the publisher nor the author shall be liable for any physical, psychological, emotional, financial, or commercial damages including but not limited to special, incidental, consequential or other damages.

PRINTED IN THE UNITED STATES OF AMERICA

Dedication

To my family

Contents

BY JOHN W. DRAWEC, ESQ

Foreword

The date was June 18, 2000. I remember it well. It was the day I transferred as a Massachusetts State Police (MSP) patrol supervisor to supervisor of the Crime Scene Services Section in Agawam (CSSS-Agawam).

Prior to that, I spent over a decade on patrol and as an instructor at the MSP Academy. I worked my way through the ranks of sergeant, to lieutenant, and then detective lieutenant. I also earned a law degree and have been an attorney in Massachusetts for over two decades.

While in Agawam, I received some of the best education and training opportunities a sworn officer could obtain. These included not only dozens of forensic classes, but also homicide school offered by the New England State Police Administrators Conference and the Advanced Homicide School at Princeton University sponsored by the New Jersey State Police.

These trainings included sessions in all aspects of homicide and forensic investigations with renowned criminalists such as Henry Lee, Peter DeForest, Michael Baden, and Cyril Wecht. My new assignment encompassed the four western counties of the Commonwealth. At times, that assignment took me to other parts of Massachusetts. One such time was nine days later, June 27, 2000.

It was a Tuesday afternoon when we received a request for assistance at an active scene in the town of Warren, approximately forty-five minutes away. Located in Worcester County, the town was covered by the MSP crime scene unit in Devens. They had requested assistance from Agawam because several areas needed processing. Two of us headed to Warren, an old mill town that once housed a textile plant and not much else. It was an area I knew well, having grown up in neighboring Palmer.

Upon arrival, we were briefed on details. A sixteen-year-old lifeguard named Molly Bish was missing from her post at Comins Pond. They first believed she may have drowned, but a search of the pond revealed nothing. Other scenarios were playing out. Did she run away, or was this a possible abduction?

It's the latter scenario that put everyone on edge. This was small town America, and abductions weren't supposed to happen here. People were worried. I knew most of the officers at the scene and could see the concern on their faces.

I soon found out that this was metaphorically family for us, as Molly's father was a probation officer in a nearby court. I didn't realize it at the time, but I was just called into what would turn out to be one of the most highly publicized cases in Massachusetts history.

Days, weeks, months, and years have passed since that day. Over time, the MSP resources were utilized to their maximum potential on this case. The state police academy was two towns away, and hundreds of trainees helped in the searches. The MSP Air Wing flew numerous missions, K-9 searches were conducted, and hundreds of interviews have taken place.

Nearly three years later, we received a second request for assistance from the Devens unit. Molly Bish's remains had been found on Whiskey Hill in Palmer. I sent two troopers to help.

Whiskey Hill sits in an area where three towns come together, Palmer, Ware and Warren. Molly's remains were found in Palmer, which is part of Hampden County. Ware sits in Hampshire County, while Warren is in Worcester County. This put the scene of Molly's remains squarely in the middle of a jurisdictional nightmare.

In Massachusetts, the district attorney of jurisdiction oversees all death investigations, yet Molly's case surprisingly remained with the Worcester County DA's office. The case of Holly Piirainen who also went missing from Worcester and found in Hampden County, is under the direction of the Hampden County DA's office.

At the scene of Molly's remains in Palmer, I witnessed firsthand the meticulous processing the site endured over several days. Years later, I saw a clip on the national news showing an individual, who was at the scene with the news crew, reach down and pick up a fabric scrap purported to be a piece of Molly's bathing suit. The fabric was laying on top of leaves.

Layers of leaves are an effective cover, especially year after year in New England. Knowing how meticulously Molly's scene was processed all those years earlier, I questioned how a scrap of fabric could be laying in plain view on top of forest debris three years later.

In 2009, I had the opportunity to head a college forensic science program. I said goodbye to my position at MSP, and hello to forensics and academia. For the next ten years, I taught and mentored students who are now forensic scientists throughout the United States, many in Massachusetts. I always stressed that integrity in forensic science is paramount. Some of those students now work in death penalty jurisdictions where there is zero room for error and the need for utmost integrity.

A crime scene is like putting together a puzzle. In a traditional puzzle, you first look at the picture. You know the number of pieces. You find the edge pieces, build the frame, and then interlock all the inner pieces according to color and shape.

A crime scene is a different kind of puzzle, yet the principle is the same. The pieces are individual evidentiary items. Recognition is key. Could it be evidence? Think outside the box. If the answer is yes, it must be documented, collected, processed and analyzed as a potential piece as evidence.

The challenge is that a crime scene puzzle has no picture, no shape and no straight edges to start. Some pieces may be missing and others don't belong. The number of pieces is unknown, yet we seek to form a clear picture of interlocking pieces that create a complete story from individual points of interest. It's not an easy task.

While teaching, I served on the university's selection committee for a tenure-track position for a criminal justice professor. Our search process narrowed down two candidates who were both favorable and equal yet had different backgrounds. One of the two candidates was Dr. Sarah L. Stein.

Sarah was a professor at a university outside Atlanta. She was of special interest because not only did she hold a doctorate degree in criminal justice, she also had a master's degree in forensic science, and I needed help with my growing forensic science program.

The committee recommended both candidates, and both were offered positions with the stipulation that Sarah could teach lab sessions for introductory forensic science.

Soon after she was hired, I learned Sarah had consulted with the Bish family. I confided that Molly's case was the first homicide I was called in to assist with at Agawam. It was apparent that Sarah wasn't a fan of the Massachusetts State Police. I took offense at first, but soon realized that she had dealt with only a few MSP detectives. They aren't known for seeking outside help, and some are easier to work with than others.

Sarah is a brilliant woman and an authority in unresolved cases. I have read her material, seen her teach class, and listened to her speak. She is recognized in the U.S. and abroad as someone with a knack for investigative preciseness.

Both of us had weathered the dissolution of a marriage, and we became good friends. I soon noticed Sarah's devotion both to the Bish family and Molly's case. Many times she would suddenly stop what she was doing to jot something down in a journal, explaining that it had to do with Molly's case and she didn't want to forget to follow up on whatever it was. Over time, I started assisting Sarah with some of those activities, got to know the Bish family personally, and attended some of the vigils.

This book is the account of Sarah's journey to assist the Bish family in finding out exactly what happened and who was responsible for Molly's abduction and murder. Sarah has devoted years of her life, thousands of dollars of her own funds, and many tears as she sought justice for Molly. She never billed a single penny in all the years she consulted on Molly's case.

Sarah and I are now married, and I can say unequivocally that she is driven, focused and thorough. I watched her pass along information freely to the MSP without getting anything in return. Her dedication is unparalleled.

Some of my former MSP colleagues are also the best at what they do. They took their job as investigators with equal rigor and fight, but I also know they couldn't devote all their time to one case. Another case comes in before you can finish the first, and then another. I lived that reality.

Sarah's story is a humbling and honest reflection of nearly fifteen years of dedication and loyalty in the pursuit for justice for an innocent victim, and to complete the full picture of that elusive puzzle all good investigators seek.

JOHN W. DRAWEC, ESQ.

BY SARAH L. STEIN

Introduction

My name is Sarah L. Stein, and this is the story of how I came to know Molly and her life, of how my own life was shaped by her disappearance and murder, and how I came to know what I believe to be the truth, or rather pieces thereof, of what happened to Molly on that fateful day of June 27, 2000.

I did not record this journey because I wanted to. Putting these words down on paper is exposing my soul. It is the opus of half a lifetime's work, encapsulated by memories of love, fear, excitement, anguish, persistence, and hope. I am sharing this journey with you because I made a promise to Molly, her family, the many communities affected, and to myself to find the person responsible for the abduction and murder of Molly Ann Bish from Warren, Massachusetts.

The truth on the following pages is my own, and only mine. It is not Molly's, her family's, nor the truth of the many communities, agencies, and individuals who helped Molly's case over the years. I wrote this story to raise awareness about protocols used by our criminal investigation systems in the United States, and the responses to incidences of missing persons and cold cases.

Perhaps you are a true crime fan, an armchair detective, or in law enforcement. You may be a family member of a murder victim, or a student in criminal justice. Whatever your background, whatever your motivation for reading this is—please know that this is my truth.

While I never intended to write about Molly, or my involvement in her case, I had to show through my eyes what families of missing or murdered victims must endure, and how justice has failed them.

I am not sharing my story for profit. All profit will be donated to the advancement of law enforcement training as well as legislative efforts to help improve the handling of unresolved cases and missing persons in the United States.

As you read this story, you might get the impression that I'm not supportive of law enforcement and their efforts. This is the antithesis of how I feel. In almost twenty years in this field, most law enforcement I've consulted for are consummate professionals, dedicated, and kind. In fact, many in the law enforcement community whom I have met are not unlike myself—they keep photos of their bottom-drawer case on their desk. The term "bottom-drawer" is used for those cases an investigator is particularly attached to. They mourn the victim for whom they seek justice and carry a bottomless pit of passion to fight for resolution. In Molly's investigation, many of those I worked with met this description. Yet, as in any profession, several did not.

At the outset of my involvement in Molly's case, I was at best considered a nuisance; at worst, a liability to be controlled by the Massachusetts State Police, who considered me a young girl with no training or credibility.

I got my training. I also earned my credibility. Yet, the work I was asked to do by Molly's family was ignored by MSP. While detectives happily took information I provided, they gave absolutely none to me in return. While they weren't obligated to do so, the lack of information and communication made my job that much harder.

Even worse was that the MSP gave minimal information to the Bish family, even though the Massachusetts Victim Bill of Rights[1] obligates them to do so.

One can easily run through a list of reasons why information might be withheld from a family. Maybe certain suspects haven't yet been ruled out, or they don't want to get the family's hopes up until they know whether a lead is viable. Both reasons are valid. Yet the treatment of victims' families can make or break their resilience to survive losing a loved one in such a horrific manner.

I wasn't alone in my struggle for information. The Massachusetts State Police was awarded The Golden Padlock in 2015 by Investigative Reporters and Editors, Inc. (IRE)[2] as the most secretive agency in the United States. The IRE stated, "The Massachusetts State Police habitually go to extraordinary lengths to thwart public records requests, protect law enforcement officers and public officials who violate the law, and block efforts to scrutinize how the department performs its duties. It normally takes months or longer to respond to news media Freedom of Information requests. Requests for basic documents routinely produce refusals, large portions of blacked out documents or demands for tens of thousands of dollars in unjustified fees."[3]

I have enormous respect and gratitude for the women and men in blue across the United States. They put their own lives on the line between criminals and the innocent every day, and live with tremendous stress, both physical and mental, and often sacrifice their own wellbeing for the safety of others.

We expect these individuals to be subjected to some of the most heinous scenes a human can observe, and then return to duty and their families seemingly unscathed. This is fundamentally impossible, and yet suicide, PTSD, hypertension, alcohol and drug abuse all remain muted conversations. Those officers who do seek treatment are commonly perceived as weak, and risk being ostracized by and from fellow officers. This is our failure as a society.

What I take exception to in my story are those who become an officer because they want a badge, a gun, and control.

I have a duty to Molly, myself, and society to raise awareness, open the dialogue, and improve the way investigations are handled. It's our societal duty to be the voice for those who no longer have one. I pray this story will inspire others to become a catalyst for change.

SARAH L. STEIN, PH.D.

CHAPTER ONE

Ouroboros

On June 27, 2000, at 10 a.m. in Warren, Massachusetts, sixteen-year-old Molly Ann Bish was kidnapped from her lifeguard post at a local pond. To this day, I don't know why I lived and why Molly was taken. Further, I don't know why the universe intertwined our fates, but such was my path.

That same day at 4 p.m. I was in Paris, getting my first tattoo. I was seventeen and had chosen the image of the ouroboros. A symbol of the self in psychology, it's a snake seemingly devouring its own tail, representing the ever-renewing soul.

I do not know why I am choosing to write this now. Perhaps it is cathartic to tell my truth. Perhaps it is my duty, or an amalgamation. As the twentieth anniversary of Molly's abduction and murder nears, I hope this book will help produce the final piece in the elusive puzzle of Molly's investigation. I also hope readers will become more aware of failures in aspects of the U.S. criminal justice system.

Molly changed me. And I, her family, her town, and many others through persistence, stumbles, and eventually a life-altering journey into some of the darkest places I have ever visited, metaphorically and physically.

I do not presume to tell Molly's story, nor do I have the arrogance to assume I know the complete truth of Molly's investigation. The words I pen are my truths—my experiences, and what I know to be real in my heart.

This is the story of how Molly Bish changed my life after nearly fifteen years of searching for and, I believe, finding her killer who was never brought to justice.

I was in my senior year of high school when I first read about Molly. "No New Clues in Search for Missing Lifeguard," said the head-line. I saw her face. Delicate, yet strong. Her eyes, shy yet bold. Her style was all-American—plaid shirt and blue jeans. The smile on her face? Haunting. I felt a tug in my chest. And then a schoolboy I liked asked me to the fall dance, and Molly became a ghost of a memory for the time being.

Figure 1: Molly's buttons from her 15th anniversary.

Molly would have turned eighteen on August 2, 2001. Her family held a vigil to commemorate the 500 days she had been missing.

2

Two and a half years later, the family marked 1,000 days. They also designated a symbol to recognize Molly: the dragon-fly, signifying transformation.

In August 2001, I began my under-graduate studies at American University in Washington, D.C. The next year while taking a criminal justice course, we were asked to research an unsolved case that interested us.

Figure 2: The button commem-orating the 1,000 days Molly had been missing.

I chose twelve-year-old Ashley Pond, who disappeared on her way to school on the morning of January 9, 2002, in Oregon. Two months later, on March 8, her friend, Miranda Gaddis, also disap-peared on the way to school. Both girls lived in the same apartment complex, attended the same school, participated on the same dance team, and took the same route to the school bus. A possible connection could not be ignored.

While researching the case, I connected both with reporters and authorities in Oregon. One source suggested I call the girls' neighbor, Ward Weaver. His daughter was friends with both girls.

I called Mr. Weaver, and was surprised when he returned my call. As a nineteen-year-old college student, I hadn't expected him to. Why would a fifty-something year-old man return a call from a college girl? Further, why would he talk with me for over two hours about the missing girls, how much he cared for them, how much his own

3

daughter missed them, and how he would do anything to help? It turns out that Weaver was the killer. At the time, I didn't know that certain typologies of killers tend to interject themselves whenever possible. I do now.

During my research, I discovered Weaver's father was on death row at San Quentin prison for abducting, murdering, and then burying a young woman in his backyard. When I asked Weaver about his father over the phone, his mask of congeniality was replaced with rage. He vehemently denied being anything like his father and berated me for daring to bring up his past. That was the last time we talked. I contacted the FBI and told them about my conversation with Weaver.

I began getting hang-up calls on the eighth and ninth of each month, the days Miranda and Ashley disappeared.

In July, authorities could not locate Weaver and believed he may have fled. I was in a summer course when the FBI called my cellphone in the middle of class. The professor was livid. "Who is that?!"

"Um, it's the FBI."

The professor called my bluff, took my phone and after a short conversation, handed it back. I took the call out in the hall.

In August, Weaver sexually assaulted and attempted to murder his son's girlfriend. She had a child with Weaver's son, and during the assault, pleaded with him, "Think of what this'll do to your grandson!"

Weaver hesitated briefly, giving her an opportunity to flee naked into the street, to safety. This gave authorities the probable cause they needed to search Weaver's property.

While investigators combed the scene, community mourners began to gather at the site. The chain-link fence surrounding the crime scene was soon overtaken with flower bouquets, letters, and stuffed animals.

Figure 3: Weaver's property.

The end result was dismal. Ashley's remains were recovered from a fifty-gallon drum buried beneath a concrete slab. Miranda's remains were found in a large box at the back of the property. Weaver's house was later demolished.

It was eventually discovered that Weaver himself was just nine years old when he helped his father dig the grave for his father's victim, thus psychologically grooming Weaver to replicate the crime later in his own life.

Figure 4: The girls' yearbook.

It was also discovered that Weaver had been sexually abusing Ashley. She told authorities but her report went uninvestigated by the Department of Human Services. [4]

Weaver then killed her.

Ashley's mother hired a private forensic K-9 unit to search Weaver's property. The dogs alerted to something suspicious, and an extensive report was sent to the FBI,[5] and either could not be used or was simply ignored.

Miranda's death came because of her love for her friend. On the morning of March 8, Weaver convinced Miranda that Ashley had returned home but was hurt and needed Miranda.

Miranda then disappeared.

Weaver later said he killed Miranda because he feared she had seen him disposing of Ashley's body.

Both deaths may have been preventable. In the aftermath of the investigations into the girls' disappearances, I decided this was what I wanted to do with my life—help address failures in our criminal justice system and resolve investigations.

I lost my own mother when I was four. Adopted by my maternal grandmother and step-grandfather, I refer to them as my parents, as that is what they are. I love them with all my heart, yet I myself, in many ways, was a lost child. Perhaps that is the individuating aspect that led me to this work: I wanted to protect other children.

Figure 5: Dr. Stein at age 4 kneeling over her mother's headstone with her maternal grandmother.

I designed my own major entitled, "The Victimology of Pedophilia." Victimology is the study of a victim while pedophilia is the disorder that causes individuals to have sexual preference for prepubescent children. My major drew from the fields of criminal justice, sociology, and psychology.

Early in my career, I began teaching that if you know your victim, you will know your perpetrator. In Ashley and Miranda's case, Ashley herself held the reason why Weaver murdered her—she was going to tell about the sexual abuse.

For Miranda, Weaver knew that her love for her friend would outweigh any concern for herself. If you know your victim, you know your perpetrator.

A year later, on June 9, 2003, I was well into my studies when another CNN headline appeared, something to the effect of "Missing Lifeguard's Remains Identified." There was Molly in her plaid shirt and blue jeans with her haunting, knowing smile and, as her mother Magi often called them, cornflower-blue eyes.

A rush of memories flooded back to me. That moment in high school when I saw Molly for the first time, what I was wearing, where I was sitting, and the cute boy who asked me to the dance.

The tug in my heart grew stronger. I left a simple note on the family's website identifying myself and my studies in school, offering whatever assistance I could.

On December 3, 2003, my phone rang. "Sarah? Someone named John Bish for you?"

Molly's father. My fate had called.

[JOURNAL ENTRY]

01/05/04

Several weeks ago (December 3, 2003) I received a call from John Bish, father to Molly Ann Bish. Mr. Bish asked if I would share my thoughts with him about Molly's abduction and her assailant.

CASE HISTORY:

Molly Ann Bish – DOB: August 2, 1983

Molly was 16 at the time of her disappearance. She had recently taken a summer job as a lifeguard at Comins Pond in Warren, MA. The day she was abducted was her 8th day on the job. Molly's mother, Magi, had made a habit out of dropping her daughter off at approximately 9:45 every morning. The day before Molly's disappearance, Magi dropped her daughter off as usual, except there was a man lurking in a white car that seemed suspicious. He was smoking a cigarette, appeared to be in his early to mid-fifties, had salt-and-pepper hair, and was heavy set. Mrs. Bish then waited until he was gone to leave Molly for work. On June 9, 2003, Molly's remains were found five miles away from her abduction site, on Whiskey Hill in Palmer, Massachusetts. Only partial remains were recovered.

THE CRIME SCENES:

1. Site of Abduction:

a.   Comins Pond, where Molly was abducted, is a small, local water hole where neighborhood children take swimming lessons in the summer. All that was left of Molly at the pond was her police radio, *open* first aid kit, beach towel, water bottle, her sandals, and lunch. It is my deduction that the assailant approached Molly for help, asking for a Band-Aid, etc. Once she bent to get the item, he grabbed her.

The path that bloodhounds caught Molly's scent on is dense with brush and twigs. She never would have gone willingly up that path without shoes.

2. **Site Where Remains Were Recovered:**

a. It could be assumed that the killer intentionally looked for higher ground so that he could detect if anyone was coming. However, sounds travel farther from elevated ground and he must have known that Molly's screams could be heard. This leads me to four possible conclusions:

    i. He knew neither of these facts and the spot was coincidental

    ii. He gagged Molly

    iii. He had a weapon with which to keep her quiet via coercion

    iv. Whiskey Hill was somehow otherwise significant to him (near Sportsmen's Club)

Profile of the killer:

He is extremely antisocial. He most likely has a job with a low level of interaction with others such as a laborer, factory, or construction worker. He is or was at one time a local resident. Other kidnapping cases with similar M.O.s (Modus Operandi) of stalking locally and out of state should be examined. He is also extremely cocky: he wanted Magi to see his face – power and control, torment.

Figure 6: Comins Pond, Warren, MA, 2004.

CHAPTER TWO

Commitment

[JOURNAL ENTRY]

May 7, 2004

Confirmed yesterday, May 6, with John Bish via telephone that I would be coming to Warren. Dates: May 15 – May 17 (Saturday–Monday). Driving Time: 6 hrs. 50 min. Items Needed: Latex gloves, camera/film, paper and plastic bags, 4 tapes, and batteries for tape recorder.

John Bish invited me to meet his family and begin volunteering with them. My parents insisted I get a new cellphone before I made the journey from Washington, D.C. to Warren, Massachusetts, in my silver Volkswagen Beetle.

It was the days of Mapquest, Nokia phones, and blissful college whimsy when I didn't yet know who I was, yet was still firm with resolution that one day, some way, I might change the world.

I printed out directions to Warren, an approximately six-and-a-half-hour drive. I got snacks, sodas, change for tolls, my CD case, my suitcase, Nokia phone, and everything an amateur sleuth would need: binoculars, a notebook, pens, and tape recorder. I had no idea what I was getting into. Undaunted and naïve as hell, I was about to embark on a trek that would change my future.

After the death of my mother, I was extremely sheltered as a child. The fear of losing me overshadowed everything my grandparents did. I wasn't allowed to even cross the street by myself until I was ten or so. Through high school, I had a strict curfew. So, taking a solo journey all the way from D.C. to Massachusetts was huge.

I was amped. The air was warm, my windows were down, and my tunes were cranked. Along the journey, I got stuck for two hours on the George Washington Bridge in New York. The shake of the semis passing by my little Beetle was the first test of my nerves.

[JOURNAL ENTRY]

May 15, 2004 5:11 P.M.

After a nine-hour drive, I arrived in Sturbridge, MA. I am currently waiting outside my hotel, The Comfort Inn, for Mr. Bish to pick me up. I don't think it's actually sunk in that I'm here yet. I didn't get lost on the way which shocked the heck out of me. I'm so anxious to ask all these questions and go to Comins Pond and Whiskey Hill but I've got to remember that I am dealing with Molly's father. He is such a strong person that it is difficult to envision him as a grieving parent.

I was staying at the Comfort Inn & Suites in Sturbridge, about twenty minutes outside Warren. After checking in, I sat anxiously on the bench outside the hotel, waiting for John Bish to pick me up.

I clearly remember the first time I met him. A wiry, energetic man, John had an enigmatic smile that told you he was always one step ahead and had no intention of slowing down. A gray minivan swerved into the hotel parking lot, and no sooner had the vehicle been put in park, there was John hopping out holding a cup of Dunkin Donuts coffee between his teeth. He was juggling two cellphones, one in each hand, talking to two different people. He gave me a rushed hug and said hurriedly, "Come on, sweetheart. Get in the car, we gotta go!"

I jumped in and off we went. John drove us to Springfield, an interesting city rife with gang and drug activity. It was not a place I would have ventured on my own, yet in that moment I felt brave. We arrived at a rally for crime victims held in a local park. The emotion of the crowd was raw, electric, alive, and volatile. There was unrest, pain, and anger at authorities for failing to do their jobs. It was a collective call for justice.

John was the final speaker of the rally, and he walked toward the microphone with a worn determination to once again tell the story of his Molly. A noticeable hush came over the crowd as his soft voice began, "My daughter's name is Molly Ann Bish. She was a lifeguard. She was abducted and murdered on June 27, 2000."

The story continued, spanning the three painful years between the time Molly vanished and when her bathing suit was recovered five miles from the pond by local hunter Ricky Boudreau and retired police officer Timothy McGuigan. McGuigan had asked Molly's family for permission to research her case, and possible connections to another local unsolved homicide, that of Holly Piirainen.

As the story goes, a few weeks later McGuigan was describing Molly's bathing suit to his girlfriend and her brother, Ricky. Ricky reportedly said something to the effect of, "I think I saw something like that on Whiskey Hill back in November." The two went to the hill, and lo and behold, there was the suit.

Following the discovery of the suit, Molly came home, or rather, twenty-six of her bones came home. Laid to rest in the cemetery behind the pond where she was abducted, Molly was buried in a child's casket with her favorite stuffed animal Tigger, her junior prom dress, and mementos from family and friends on what would have been her twentieth birthday, August 2, 2003[6].

As I stood there watching John speak and the crowd around him, I felt tears staining my cheeks. I felt hot, sick, and an anger foreign to me craved justice.

John walked back to me and I opened my arms. He fell into me. "I'm so sorry about Molly," I whispered as our tears dropped on the other's shoulder.

Figure 7: Molly's grandmother's headstone with a memento for Molly, who is buried next to her.

He said, "I'll take you to the pond tomorrow. Let's go get something to eat."

That night at dinner, we laughed when he ordered a cheeseburger without the cheese. He called Magi, explaining to her where we had been all day. She was expecting us to be back by early evening at the latest. He then told me a story about when Molly got her tongue pierced. It had been a reward for making honor roll her junior year. Mom was against it, Dad was all for it. The next morning, my head was spinning with way more questions than answers.

[JOURNAL ENTRY]

Sunday, May 16, 2004 9:15 A.M.

Last night was phenomenal. It was the most life-changing experience I've ever had. My first impression of Mr. Bish was a bit shaky as he was on the phone when he pulled into the driveway of the Comfort Inn. The man has no sensate function whatsoever. His driving skills leave much to be desired and his Dodge van (color gray) was cluttered to the hilt. However, after coming to know him, he is a brilliant man, filled with kindness and generosity, and an overwhelming devotion to his cause.

We drove and just chitchatted about school, parents, etc. I didn't want to push him too much too soon. We arrived in Springfield to participate in an event primarily geared toward ending domestic violence. We were able to photograph and fingerprint 50 children alone at this one event.

We then participated in a candlelight march/vigil within the neighborhood chanting phrases such as, "Rape is hate our community will not tolerate!" and "People unite! Take back the night!" When we arrived back at the park around 9:00 P.M. people who had lost loved ones to violence were given a chance to speak. Mr. Bish gave a very moving speech about Molly, and we both cried and hugged and held each other surrounded by poverty, despair, and a determination to change.

The profoundness of the event came upon realizing that this is how change happens, not legislation or signing the AMBER Alert Bill, but this—communities banding together to bring their children safety and a brighter future in what has become such a bleak and dark world.

We then went to dinner at a restaurant called Friendly's, the owner of which put up $10,000 to help find Molly's abductor. We had burgers, fries, and sodas and started to head back to the hotel. On the way, we drove down Five Bridge Road, where Holly Piirainen's body was found. The energy in that spot was profoundly unsettling and I could feel a distinct presence of unrest and one might even venture to say evil. This child experienced a very violent and traumatic death. I am curious to know what I will feel at the sites of Molly's abduction and murder.

The case of Holly Piirainen received disproportionate attention from the media compared to Molly's, and stories regarding Molly often referenced Holly. Further, there is an almost eerie connection between the two.

Holly was abducted on August 5, 1993, in Sturbridge, which is in Worcester County. Only her shoe was found at the abduction site. Following an intensive search, her remains were found ten weeks later by hunters on October 23, 1993. Her case remains unsolved.

Holly was a bright, vivacious, ten-year-old who loved animals and aspired to be a marine biologist. In fact, it was her love of animals that exposed her to this fate: know your victim.

On the afternoon of August 5, Holly and her younger brother walked down a secluded road to see a new litter of puppies. Only Holly's younger brother returned. Then Holly's shoe was found.

Figure 8: A cross at the location where Holly's remains were found.

The police came, the media came. MSP trooper Richard McKeon allegedly told the family at the time that they didn't need the notebook of tips the family had been compiling. This is important because in a large percentage of cold cases, the perpetrator's name can be found in the case file within the first thirty days of the investigation. Developed by Dr. Robert Keppel, one of the most brilliant minds in our field, that research was instrumental in apprehending both Ted Bundy and Gary Ridgway, The Green River Killer.

Trooper McKeon went on to be an colonel with the MSP and then retired amidst a powder keg scandal[7] alleging that the same

Figure 9: Dr. Stein's tip campaign binder.

17

district attorney responsible for Molly's investigation, Joe Early, had demanded the colonel alter the report of a judge's daughter who was arrested for driving under the influence. The report was altered, the trooper who made the arrest was disciplined for refusing to change his statement, and Colonel McKeon retired.

Joe Early was re-elected and, as of this writing, remains under investigation with the State Ethics Commission as recommended by the Attorney General for the Commonwealth of Massachusetts.[8] Further, Early and the Massachusetts State Police settled a $40,000 civil case with the trooper who was forced to change his report, $5,000 of which was personally paid by the District Attorney Joe Early.[9]

The first connection between Holly and Molly is that both girls were ten years-old in 1993. The second connection was revealed much later. Molly heard of Holly's abduction during a church service in Warren. The town priest had asked for prayers for Holly's family. Molly decided a letter was appropriate.[10]

[EXCERPT FROM MOLLY'S LETTER TO HOLLY'S FAMILY]

I am very sorry. I wish I could make it up to you. Holly is a very pretty girl. She is almost as tall as me. I wish I knew Holly. I hope they find her.

Seven years later, Molly met the same fate at Comins Pond, and I was about to see it for the first time.

Comins Pond is a spot that used to hold joy; a place for the residents of Warren to celebrate the brevity of summer in New England. Located at the end of a residential street, it is both charming and secluded.

Figure 10: The view Molly's killer was believed to have had the morning of her abduction.

As John and I pulled into the empty parking lot, I noticed yellow ribbons for Molly tied to fences and trees, floating heavily in the bated air. My breath was stuck in my chest as we stepped on to the path leading to the beach. Something would never be the same. With each step, I felt the weight, the sadness, the raw pain of this place. Though the air was warm, I was chilled.

John stopped on the bridge on the way to the beach and reached for a yellow ribbon tied to a fence pole. Gingerly, tenderly, as if he were touching Molly herself, John untied the piece of fabric and handed it gently to me. "We can't really afford to pay you anything, but I hope you remember Molly."

Tears glistened in his eyes as they met mine, my fingers closing around the ribbon. At that moment, we both understood that he was trusting me with his heart. I had just been handed the weight of the world, the responsibility of doing whatever was humanly possible to bring justice to Molly. I answered him with a promise, "Always."

From Comins Pond we went to Whiskey Hill, where Molly's remains were found. On the opposite side of the road is a hunting club. I always found that eerie. Could Molly have been considered prey?

John and I hiked up the steep hillside. As I took in the terrain around me, it did not have the same energy as Comins Pond. I did not believe Molly was murdered there. It did not make sense that a perpetrator would risk an assault and murder in woods used by hunters year round. I considered the possibility that she was murdered somewhere else, a secondary location, such as an abandoned house.

John found three large stones and made a marker on the spot where the majority of Molly's bones were recovered, and then turned to me and said, "Just in case I drop dead, you can find this place again."

I stared at the ground and surrounding area that had been sifted through by the Massachusetts State Police about a year before. Pulling the recruit class out of the academy to aid in the search, these troopers were so thorough that they allegedly found Molly's tongue ring, her present for making honor roll,[11] while Molly's family watched from the roadside, coming to the realization that this was all they had left.

On that trip, I reviewed the case with John and Magi, and we discussed logical persons of interest, some who had been named in the media, some who had not. I also began to develop my victimology report on Molly.

Molly was the youngest child of John and Magdalen "Magi" Bish. Her two older siblings are John Jr. and Heather. John Bish's parents hailed from Warren. When John and Magi were a young, married couple living in Detroit, a woman was murdered in their neighborhood, prompting them to move back to Warren, ironically thinking it would be a safe place to raise a family.

Growing up, Molly loved the outdoors. She snowboarded—once off the roof of the family home—and wanted to be a teacher like her mom. As a teen, Molly was gregarious with friends, goofy, fun, loved Adam Sandler movies and *Forrest Gump*. She was also shy around adults and deferred to authority.

Molly was also an all-star athlete, playing on soccer, basketball, and softball teams at Quaboag Regional High School. At the time of her disappearance, Molly was working two jobs so she could buy a Volkswagen Jetta. John told me of their plans to take a historical cross-country roadtrip when she graduated.

Her first job was waitressing at Howard's Drive-In, a seasonal diner in West Brookfield. She had also taken over her older brother's position as lifeguard at Comins Pond. She underwent lifeguard lessons at the YMCA in Southbridge, and her brother trained her at the pond. On just her eighth day on the job, Molly was abducted.

There are three generally accepted categories of victims, ranked according to the individual's associated risk level for becoming the victim of a violent crime: low risk, medium risk, and high risk. One example of a low-risk victim would be a married woman who does not work and has no known enemies. If the married woman is murdered, investigators would presumably start investigating individuals closest to the victim's inner circle and work their way outward. As the victim was low risk, it's more likely that she knew her killer in some capacity.

One example of high-risk victims would be sex workers, who are often the target of serial offenders. Given that their backgrounds often include poverty, domestic violence, alcohol and/or drug abuse, their families and authorities may not be overly concerned if the individual is missing. Offenders know that these victims are not considered by society, law enforcement, and the media, to have the same inherent value as a victim like Molly Bish.

For example, Gary Ridgway, America's deadliest serial murderer, was able to continue his deadly assaults on sex workers until there were forty-eight victims.[12] Ann Rule, the author who wrote "The Stranger Beside Me," about her non-romantic relationship with Ted Bundy, penned a book titled "Green River, Running Red," a true story about the Green River Killer and his victims.

In circumstances like this, with high-risk victims, investigators must approach the task of finding the killer in exactly the opposite fashion as a low-risk victim, looking to unknown suspects first. I call this the circle of trust.

LOW RISK
Inner to outer
Start inside the victim's circle and work outward.

HIGH RISK
Outer to inner
Start outside the victim's circle and work inward.

Figure 11: Dr. Sarah Stein's circle of trust diagram.

High-risk victims are more likely to have a fleeting encounter with their killer, or not know them at all prior to the attack. The difficulty in Molly's case, with her victimology specifically, is that Molly herself was initially not a high-risk victim. However, her risk level was elevated after it was determined that she had been the victim of a violent crime, given her new position as the lifeguard at Comins

Pond. She was new on the job, alone, shy around adults, deferred easily to authority, and was in a secluded location. While Molly may have had previous contact with her killer, in my opinion, it was very little before the abduction and murder.

From a suspectology perspective, it does not make sense that someone who knew Molly and wanted to do her harm would do so in a public location, at a high-risk time, and with a limited window.

Further, if Molly knew her killer, unless she was rendered unconscious at the scene of the abduction, the perpetrator would not have time to stage the crime scene before the arrival of the first witnesses.

On Monday, June 26, 2000, the day prior to the abduction, Magi and Molly drove together to the pond. As they parked, Magi noticed one other car in the parking lot, a white, boxy-shaped vehicle. The man sitting in the car appeared to be approximately forty-five to fifty-five years old. Magi described him as Caucasian with salt-and-pepper hair. He was wearing a collared shirt and smoking a cigarette. Magi remembered that the way he held his cigarette was unusual for a man—with straight fingers and the cigarette held low between them, more effeminate.

Magi said that something about the man felt off, and her instincts kicked in. His crinkled eyes looked sinister and were unduly fixated on Molly as she walked away from the car to retrieve supplies from a barn on the opposite side of the beach. Uneasy, Magi left the car as well, and followed her daughter.

As Molly arranged her belongings, Magi commented to her how pretty the pond was and yet hadn't realized there would be so many men around. Molly laughed nonchalantly, as a teenager would, reassuring her mother they were just fishermen, and there was nothing to worry about.

When Magi returned to her car, the man in the white car was still there, still smoking, still staring. Not wanting to directly confront him, Magi pretended to look for something in her vehicle until the man drove away. Unfortunately, a license plate was not recorded. Magi left shortly thereafter.

John and Magi told me they had a conversation with Molly about safety when she returned home that night, and John gave her a Kubotan stick with which to defend herself. She never had a chance.

The next morning was unusual for Molly and her family. The evening before, Molly's friend was struck by a vehicle while riding her bike. The young lady lived but was in critical condition at the time. So, on that Tuesday morning, Magi climbed into bed with Molly to wake and tell her what had happened to her friend. I know that is a moment Magi will cherish forever; the last time she got to hold her Moll in bed, breathe in her smell, feel her close, and safe.

For that reason, the two were a bit late getting on the road. Along the way, they stopped at what was then an XTra Mart in town to buy water and snacks for Molly. A grainy black and white surveillance video image timestamped 9:51 a.m. on June 27, 2000, is the last image of Molly Bish alive.

The video footage shows Molly leaning over Magi's shoulder at the counter. Molly had her hair in a half ponytail and was wearing a pink tank-top and plaid flannel boxer shorts over her blue and white one-piece bathing suit.

Figure 12: Footage released from the morning of June 27, 2000, at the Xtra Mart in Warren (Credit: WCVB News).

Magi and Molly then drove to the Warren Police Department to pick up her two-way radio. Molly was to check in every morning when she arrived. At the time, Warren did not have cellular service, so the radio was essential. On their way to the police department, Magi and Molly passed a small playground. There was a fence around the area that was being painted by Molly's younger friend, Gerard Tatro, who often visited her at the pond, as well as Parks Commissioner Ed Fett. I'm not sure if it was a honk or a wave, but either way, there was allegedly acknowledgment of seeing each other.

It is estimated that Molly arrived at Comins Pond shortly before 10 a.m. There was no white car, no sinister man lurking, or so it appeared. Magi and Molly saw only a sand truck from Beaudry's, a local company, dumping sand on the beach for the first day of swim lessons that Molly was to supervise. At the pond, Molly hopped out, kissed her mother one final time, and said, "Bye, Mom, I love you." Then, she was gone.

Three witnesses later came forward to say they saw a white car. First, near a carwash at the head of Comins Pond Road. It then came into the parking lot of Comins Pond only to turn around and leave. It was also seen parked in the cemetery at the head of the trail leading to the beach around the time of Molly's abduction. If it weren't for those three witnesses, I don't know if the white car and its suspicious occupant would have been seriously pursued.

Later in my investigation, I went to interview Mr. Beaudry, the owner of the sand truck seen on the beach that morning. As I walked up his driveway, he held up his hand. "You better not be with the Massachusetts State Police," he said harshly.

I assured him I wasn't. He proceeded to tell me that detectives had accused him of running over Molly in the parking lot with his sand truck, despite there being no forensic evidence to support their theory.

One of the last questions I asked John Bish on that first trip to Warren was, "How are you coping?"

"I'm in denial . . . I just try to stay busy," was his response.

I headed back to Washington, D.C., while John began preparing to testify before an investigative jury regarding Molly's case that had been empaneled by then district attorney John Conte.

John was slated to testify on Wednesday, May 19. Molly's sister Heather and her brother John Jr. were scheduled for the day before. The grand jury was later dismissed without an indictment.

On August 2, 2004, what would have been Molly's twenty-first birthday, I went into Georgetown. In the muggy, dizzying summer heat of Washington D.C., I had a shot of tequila for Molly, and got a dragonfly tattoo inside my ouroboros symbolizing that I would always hold a spot for her inside my soul.

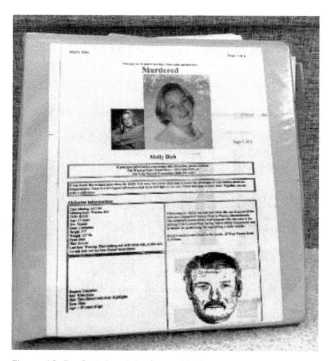

Figure 13: Dr. Stein's original case binder.

CHAPTER THREE

No lifeguard on duty

One of the biggest ironies of Molly's case has always been the fact that she was a lifeguard. Her job was to protect the lives around her, yet no one was there to protect her. The Massachusetts law has since changed following Molly's abduction to require at least two lifeguards at public beaches.

At approximately 10:15 a.m. on the morning Molly disappeared, a local mother and her children arrived at the pond for swim lessons. Molly's beach chair was set up with her sandals underneath, a Poland Springs water bottle in one of the heels. Her lifeguard whistle was wrapped around the arm of the chair and her beach towel hung over the back. Her two-way radio lay untouched and, oddly, her first-aid kit was open. Molly, however, was not there.

The mother allegedly later told retired police officer Timothy McGuigan that she observed a swath-like pattern on the hill behind the beach, as if someone had been dragged. However, that was not enough to overly concern her. She informed the parks commissioner of Molly's absence, and allegedly took Molly's whistle and assumed her duties. The parks commissioner did not report Molly missing to the Warren Police Department until approximately two hours after her disappearance.

Statistically, when a child is abducted in what is called a critical stranger incident, there is a three-hour window to find that child alive. The Warren Police Department called Magi Bish at approximately 1 p.m. to inform her that Molly was absent from her post. By the time Magi was called, in all likelihood her daughter had already been killed.

When Magi got the call regarding Molly's absence, she immediately called Molly's sister, Heather, and the two drove to the pond, first stopping at the police department and also checking with Molly's

Figure 14: Lifeguard chair at Comins Pond installed after Molly's disappearance.

friends to see if anyone had seen her. When they arrived at the pond, a Warren police officer told Magi not to worry, that Molly had probably just run off with friends. When Molly's brother heard the news, he too went to the pond. Molly's father, who was a probation officer at the time, was informed while out on a call.

At the pond, crime scene protocols initially weren't followed. Law enforcement was not yet thinking there was a crime scene to be preserved, thereby allowing dozens of well-meaning searchers to trample delicate forensic material. The scene that could have aided in the apprehension of Molly's murderer was destroyed.

As a result of Molly's case, I now teach law enforcement to use deductive logic, not inductive. I demonstrate this by using a funnel image.

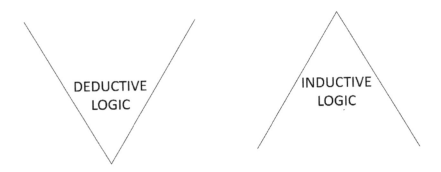

For example, if you walk into a crime scene and see a deceased man with a gunshot wound to the head and a gun in his hand, inductive logic would conclude suicide. An investigator using deductive logic would consider suicide, homicide, an accident, etc. Deductive logic will always err on the side of caution and preserve the integrity of the scene. You only have one chance to get it right.

At the time of Molly's disappearance, the Warren Police Department was about a six-man department and their initial assumption was that Molly must have simply wandered off. If that wasn't the case, she drowned. At that point, Molly's brother, John Jr., began to dive frantically into the pond searching for his sister until someone pulled him out.

Stranger abduction wasn't considered in that early critical stage of the investigation. Molly's family protested vehemently. If she wandered off or left with friends, why would her shoes still be on the beach? If she had drowned, Molly's mother argued, her shoes would be in the water. Molly never liked to venture into the pond without shoes due to the mucky bottom and leeches.

Later that day once it became apparent that Molly had not simply wandered off and that more resources were needed, the Massachusetts State Police was called in. MSP Detective Lieutenant Jack Drawec, my now retired husband, was among those who received the call for assistance. He had transferred to the Crime Scene Services unit serving the four western counties of Massachusetts just days before. Molly was his first case in his new assignment.

Even with the presence of the state police and all their resources, the family's protests that Molly hadn't wandered off or drowned went unregistered. The search for Molly that night was contained to the pond and immediate surrounding areas. The state police brought in large lights to continue their efforts.

Molly's family eventually returned home that night, where home was no longer home, but rather a place of purgatory where they prayed for the grace of God to spare them the depths of hell. Where was Molly?

Figure 15: Comins Pond equipment barn, Warren, MA, 2004.

CHAPTER FOUR

The tiny avenger

"When I first met Sarah, I thought she was a complete twit. Until I realized she knows exactly what the fuck she's doing."

This was how I was introduced to a group of police officers who attended a cold case training at the Henry C. Lee Institute at the University of New Haven. The man who delivered the backhanded compliment was Richard Walter, a dear friend and colleague.

Richard, along with two colleagues, founded The Vidocq Society, an organization that funds law enforcement agencies to come to Philadelphia once a month to present cold cases from their department. In exchange, they receive advice from the best forensic minds in the country on how to proceed with their investigation. A book was written about the legendary organization, entitled, "The Murder Room." It remained on the New York Times bestseller list for many weeks.

My parents both received doctorates from elite universities. My father, Dr. Murray Stein, is a world authority on Carl Jung, a Swiss psychiatrist and psychoanalyst contemporary to Freud. One of my father's books, "Map of the Soul," was the inspiration for the breakout K-Pop band B.T.S.'s latest album, "Map of the Soul: Persona." Their second album, based on the same text written by my father, addresses Jung's concept of the shadow, a theory that everyone is born with a dark side. If a person recognizes this and the shadow becomes conscious, an individual is considered whole and balanced.

Conversely, if this shadow is repressed, the danger for impulsive, and often criminal behavior arises. Interestingly, the general body of criminological theory essentially ignores this possibility, instead, choosing to focus on factors that lie outside of, or outside the control of an individual, such as social learning or biology.

I remember the precise moment I graduated from college. It was August 2004, one year earlier than projected. My mother and aunt came to help me decorate my apartment in Alexandria, Virginia. In between looking at decorating ideas on my laptop, I was checking emails, and received an email from American University saying I had officially graduated. My mother and aunt congratulated me, yet I opted against a formal celebration because graduate school was next. But what to study, and where? That was the big question.

When I was ten, I found "The Silence of the Lambs" in my parents' secret movie closet. I read on the VHS cover that it was about a serial killer and FBI agent, and had to watch it. That night, I announced I wanted to be an FBI agent. My dad laughed heartily, and said, "Oh, Pear, you will *never* be able to work for a bureaucracy."

How right he was. I'm a bull in a china shop in the sense that when I do a job, I do it in constant competition with myself. Even though that same drive got me perfect scores in my doctoral studies, it did not serve me well in a profession where some people in positions of power would view this dedication as a threat to their authority.

When I was eleven, my father was invited to lecture in China and Japan. My mother and I joined him. I was overwhelmed immediately—I found the mass of people and chaos terrifying. Worse still was having to wear a mask because of the smog, exaggerating what would become a lifelong struggle with claustrophobia. I will remember that trip for the rest of my life.

We ate dinner in the Forbidden City, drank frothed green tea at ancient temples in Kyoto, Japan, and enjoyed plum-filled pastries. We visited the Great Wall, and at one hotel in China, met a group of American women who were there to adopt unwanted baby girls from a culture who valued sons.

As a child, my mother always made sure I looked elegant, which I appreciate today but not when I was eleven. I was wearing a blue and white romper with nylons, and white patent leather shoes when we visited the Great Wall of China. An elderly Chinese man sitting on the wall offered to read my face. My face? My parents enthusiastically agreed, and we all sat cross-legged in a circle on the wall amid swirling August dust.

Although a stranger, I was wonderfully comfortable with him, which is very unusual for me. His eyes were bottomless and hid nothing. I could see his soul. His wrinkled hands reached for my face, and I felt a little crackle of energy as his palms cupped my cheeks. His eyes burned into mine, laser focused. Through a translator, he said, "By the time you are twenty-eight, you will have your own company, and you will go into science to catch criminals."

He was right on both counts.

I knew I didn't want to be a police officer, but not because I didn't want to serve my community. I didn't want to hold the emotional weight of having the capacity and authority to take another human life. I knew I didn't want to work in a lab, nor a routine nine-to-five job. I had to create my own career.

Thanks to John Bish writing a letter in support of my abilities, I spent the summer of 2004, as an intern for the National Center for Missing & Exploited Children. I was first assigned to conduct NCIC clearances of resolved runaway cases and then transferred to a section tasked with sending free software to law enforcement agencies that demonstrated how to make a proper missing person's poster. It was a firsthand view of what I consider reckless government spending.

At the end of the summer, interns were asked to stand and give a talk on what and how much they had learned during their time with the center. I finished my internship with the following words. "Thank you so very much for this opportunity. Thank you for showing me the truth of how much work there actually is to be done on missing persons and cold cases; work that needs to be done in the right way."

It was a bold statement for a twenty-one-year-old, yet I still believe it to this today. The politicization and handling of many cases is abysmal, though has improved somewhat with the AMBER Alert and similar legislative efforts.

At the culmination of summer, I was angry and knew I wanted to make changes in the system. I also knew I wanted to find the person who murdered Molly Bish. I considered applying to the University of New Haven for a master's in forensic science. It was a start.

[JOURNAL ENTRY]

10/18/04 8:00 P.M.

I spoke with John Bish today. He continues to be extremely busy, working 3-4 ID events every day. He is apparently as disgruntled with the NCMEC (National Center for Missing & Exploited Children) as I am, though for different reasons. Every year, the center holds a conference on missing and exploited children. This year I believe the theme was endangered runaways. At any rate, it is customary for the center to invite high profile families to the conference, and the center did not have the courtesy, nor the respect, to invite the Bish family. The blatant disrespect for families who have endured this type of tragedy is unacceptable. I was honored when John Bish told me that he carried my paper with him to some events. He also encouraged me to pursue my application to the University of New Haven for a master's in forensic science. Molly's case continues to plague and frustrate me. I feel as if there is a piece of this puzzle staring at me in the face and I fail to see it. John may be coming to D.C. at the end of October for a workshop with the DOJ (Department of Justice).

After Molly disappeared, the Molly Bish Foundation was formed over a kitchen table. For the first two weeks into the investigation of Molly's disappearance, the Massachusetts State Police sequestered the family in their home. They were ordered not to speak to the media.

[JOURNAL ENTRY]

10/23/05 11:20 P.M.

The police had instructed her and John not to talk to the media as it might anger the perp and he would hurt Molly. So, for two weeks they remained silent. Tonight, Magi sobbed, "I just keep thinking, what if, what if he had her and was hurting her for two weeks and we didn't do anything?!"

In the early phases of the investigation, law enforcement was exploring whether Molly had run away. In fact, investigators pursued this line of thinking until the very end of 2003. At the beginning of the case, it was discovered Molly made a phone call to a friend in Florida before she disappeared, so the MSP considered it a logical place she would run to. In fact, they were preparing to deploy troopers to Florida, as two unrelated witnesses had called in and said they had seen Molly. And then Molly's bathing suit was found on Whiskey Hill by McGuigan and Boudreau.

They were also closely examining Molly's new boyfriend, Steven Lukas, and his inner group of friends. Steven had had a crush on Molly since the third grade. They started dating three months prior to her abduction, and Steven took Molly to junior prom.

Molly's family was somewhat cautious about her dating Steven, as his family history was somewhat complicated. While his involvement in her disappearance is possible, it is highly unlikely. He was allegedly still asleep when someone went to his home to ask if he had seen Molly. Steven also went to the pond when the search for Molly was going on. Steven is now deceased, one of many eerie deaths surrounding Molly's investigation.

If what Magi told me was true, the advice from law enforcement would have been prudent for an inexperienced juvenile offender. An influx of intense media scrutiny would almost certainly prompt a novice criminal to cross the threshold of violence and escalate into a murderer out of fear.

Conversely, not speaking to the media did a great disservice to the investigation, as all evidence of involvement by a juvenile offender pointed to the contrary. The scene itself was organized; little to no evidence left behind, and a clean abduction in under fifteen minutes at around 10 a.m. on a Tuesday.

Further, if Molly went with Steven willingly, why not take her shoes? This is not the work of a teenager. If law enforcement had behavioral experts immediately available, this advice may very well have been revoked, and the outcome of Molly's case may have been different.

When Molly went missing, the family did not have a great photo of her head and shoulders to give to law enforcement. Nor did they have her fingerprints or a DNA sample. Molly was born in 1983, just before the era of DNA. Further, no one expected a child abduction in a rural town such as Warren. Sadly, such areas are where sexual predators flourish, as country living often translates to an everyone knows everyone mentality, unlocked doors, and an even greater potential for grave danger, simply because no one sees it coming and by the time it happens, it's too late. This is exactly what happened in Molly's case, the result being a phantom in a white car, and a frantic search for a daughter, sister, aunt and friend.

Molly's family was determined from the outset of her disappearance that this cruel fate should never befall another family. The Molly Bish Foundation's initial purpose was to host identification events. At these events, volunteers took head and shoulders photos of children along with their fingerprints, and sent them home with the parents to have on hand should the worst happen.

Before its eventual recreation into The Molly Bish Center for the Protection of Children & the Elderly, the foundation provided over 50,000 identification kits to the children of the Commonwealth of Massachusetts and their families.[13]

[JOURNAL ENTRY]

10/29/04 11:03 P.M.

Quote of the Trip: "Yeah, I watch a lot of SpongeBob" – John Bish on television shows that don't require too much thinking. I just got back from having dinner with John Bish. He flew in last night from Hartford, CT to attend a conference with the Department of Justice. I picked him up at Reagan Airport at approximately 10:00 P.M. and drove him to his hotel, The Ritz Carlton on 22nd Street NW in D.C. We got dinner at McDonald's and wandered around the city until about 12:30. Apparently the State Police found out he hired a P.I. to look into Molly's case the day he left and all hell broke loose, so the family dynamics aren't all that great right now. This afternoon we went to the Native American museum that recently opened in D.C., then had dinner at The Grill in the Ritz. During dinner, John said, "You know I never wished for this. The second I could go back to living my normal life I would...but in between we're going to fight like hell, because it's a war."

In addition to myself, John enlisted the help of former police chief Tom Shamshak to assist with Molly's investigation. A retired law enforcement professional with over twenty-one years of service including two stints as police chief, Shamshak now operated Shamshak Investigative Services out of Boston, and specialized in cold cases. The family, while certainly grateful for the efforts of both local and state police, felt that additional sets of eyes may be beneficial.

It was Shamshak who produced one of the most promising persons of interest in Molly's investigation: Rodney Stanger, who strongly resembled the sketch of the stranger in the car. A hunter and fisherman, Stanger was from Southbridge, Massachusetts. The most compelling information that led Stanger to be a person of interest was that he brutally murdered his girlfriend, Crystal Morrison, just days after she allegedly asked her sister Bonnie Kiernan, over the phone, "What's your bird's name again?"

"Molly," answered Bonnie.

Chrystal allegedly whispered, "Murders," and hung up.[14]

I'll tell you more about Stanger in a bit. In between working two jobs in Alexandria, I continued to work on Molly's case. Late in the evenings, I would sometimes find myself penning notes to Molly.

[JOURNAL ENTRY]

11/16/04 10:22 P.M.

Dear Molly,

I am sitting here in my apartment, smoking a Marlboro Light, listening to "Everything" by Lifehouse, and listening to the sound of the yellow ribbon your Poppy gave me at Comins Pond thump against the wall, blown by my ceiling fan. I marvel every day at the strength of your family. I know you are with them all the time, that you are their protector. I hope I will come to share some of that task with you.

I am trying, perhaps not hard enough, to help you and your family. I lie awake at night and wonder why these awful things happen. I think of your incredible courage and bravery. I know how hard you must have fought to get away, to keep your life. Perhaps we are the same that way; both of us are burdened with guilt, that we did not fight hard enough, do enough. I can assure you that you did.

You were, you are so brave Molly. I hope I can be as brave as you, fight as hard as you. I promise, I swear I will do everything I can to help you find your way, help your family, and hunt this bastard down.

[JOURNAL ENTRY]

12/2/04

Dear Molly,

It has been a year now, that I have tried to find your killer. I am sitting on the banks of the Potomac, watching the sun sit on the tranquil waters. I watch fish come to the surface in search of food, the ripples gliding gently to the shore, searching for contact, only receding when they have found it. If only you would seek me out this way, reach out to me, tell me who brought you to this peril. Molly, I swear to you that I will not give up this fight. I will find the person who did this to you.

The ripples on the surface of the water pass over and through each other, continuing on, unwitting participants in an elaborate game of fate. Perhaps it is so with you and me. Maybe somehow, we were destined to cross paths. Would we have been friends had we met? I think so. I wish you were here with me now, to guide me, tell me where to go or what to look for. I wish for your help, and know that it is you who needs my help, not the other way around. I swear I'll never give up, just promise me that you won't either.

That winter, I came down with a horrible case of bronchitis. To make matters worse, the heating system in my apartment building busted. One night, with my chest hurting from coughing, I sat in a hot bath for hours trying to get my fever to break. It was miserable.

One day when I had returned home from picking up medication, I found a huge bouquet of beautiful flowers at my door wrapped in cellophane, with a copy of the animated film "Ice Age" tucked inside, as well as a card.

[NOTE FROM JOHN & MAGI]

Feel better soon! Molly's case is the nut, and you're Scrat! Go get 'em!

Love,
John & Magi

If you've watched the movie "Ice Age" and its sequels, Scrat is a squirrel who is constantly trying to hunt down a single acorn. His drive is unrelenting. That gesture meant the world to me, and that reputation would follow me throughout my work on Molly's case.

I was then accepted into the Master of Forensic Science Program at the University of New Haven. I had a choice between two tracks: criminalistics or advanced investigation. I chose the latter. In January of 2005, I made another trip to Warren.

[JOURNAL ENTRY]

1/28/05 10:10 A.M.

I am sitting in John and Magi Bish's living room. Morning sunlight is streaming through crimson and white gossamer curtains, transforming the light in the room to an amber rose hue. Celine Dion's "A Mother's Prayer" is playing softly in the background. As I hear the melancholy notes of the music and sit in John's armchair nestled in this cozy light, I feel as if I have slipped from the real world. I feel as though I've been whisked away to a secret haven sustained only by memories of distant laughter and childhood smiles. What remains of the physical world reflects the hearts of the living: chaotic, overwhelmed, grief stricken. There is clutter all about; Molly is everywhere. She sits across from me now, leaned gingerly in a faded silver frame against the fireplace. Her cornflower blue eyes glitter with the anticipation of life that seems to come naturally at sixteen. Her honey hair falls over her bare shoulders and her smile is wide and captivating, unrestrained.

Last night as we drove, Mick and John chatted in the back while Magi drove, and I stroked her shoulder as she cried. The night is a cloak that hides her anguished tears. "A Mother's Prayer" played in the crowded minivan as we drove past the Nenameseck Sportsmen's Club. Magi unconsciously flooded the darkened tree line with her brights, as if still searching for her Moll, or perhaps simply lending her a light so she may find her way home. This existence is bittersweet and somehow beautiful and haunting.

There is a wall in Molly's room downstairs that John cannot bring himself to paint. It is covered with Molly's art: flowers, suns, smiley faces. There are a good twenty phone numbers and names etched into the wood, and phrases like "DIET" and "LIFE SUCKS" in true adolescent form. How could this man see Molly, and even dare to think she could be his? How, in a single moment, could he, without

47

remorse, snatch away the pillar upon which a family's foundation was based? Moreover, how could he remain silent, observing the Bishs enduring, soul shattering agony, year after year? I will never understand.

Another particularly moving yet horrifying portion of that trip was going to an interpretive performance arranged by a local dance troupe in John and Magi's honor. We walked into a room decorated in soft pink and purple lighting. Scarves hung from the ceilings and eerie music played in the background. It looked like the scene from a deranged carnival fun house.

I can't remember the exact title of the performance, but the theme throughout was a mother being separated from her daughter. They were dancing out Molly's abduction, thinking that somehow this would be a beautiful tribute to Molly and her family.

The dancer playing the part of the mother was reaching out desperately to her child, while the dancer who played the daughter was seemingly being pulled away by an unseen actor. Magi was sitting beside me coming unraveled, clutching my hand, her other hand over her heart, and tears were streaming down her face. It's interesting to me what some people think is kind.

While returning to John and Magi's house after the unnerving performance, I fell asleep in the backseat, having forgotten to buckle my seatbelt. All of a sudden, the brakes slammed and I went flying. John and Magi's arms went across the space between their seats and I crashed into them instead of the windshield. We were there for each other when it was life or death, triumph or defeat. We remained hopeful, even if death and defeat seemed to be the likely outcomes.

During the summer of 2005, I prepared to move to New Haven. I picked out an apartment, got my fall schedule of courses, and secured an internship with Congresswoman Rosa DeLauro with hopes of advancing my knowledge of politics within the criminal justice system. I also attended my first Ride for Molly, a benefit for the Molly Bish Foundation, my first of many vigils to commemorate Molly.

[JOURNAL ENTRY]   7/31/05

I went to Warren on June 25 – 28. I participated in The Ride for Molly and got a killer burn on my left calf from a motorcycle muffler. Over 1,300 riders came. It was unbelievable. I got to ride with Magi and her sisters in a convertible. All along the route, supporters stood outside their homes, clapping and cheering, displaying signs with words of encouragement for the Bish family. The next day was the five-year anniversary of Molly's abduction and murder. There was a candlelight vigil and ceremony by sunset on the town common, followed by a walk to Comins Pond where we placed lanterns in the shape of lotus blossoms in the water while the highland bagpipers played a lullaby as darkness fell. It was unbelievably moving. I had a chance to meet Tom Shamshak, Tim McGuigan, and Kim Ring (local reporter). Tom, John, and I went to Whiskey Hill as well. Dr. Ann Marie Mires (forensic anthropologist) was able to pinpoint the exact spot where Molly was originally left. We also put a white cross commemorating Molly's life on the hill in an impromptu roadside service blessed by the town priest.

Figure 16: Whiskey Hill where some of Molly's remains were recovered.

During my studies at the University of New Haven, I earned a few nicknames among faculty members including "Elle Woods of Forensic Science." I like pink and loved the movie, but my favorite nickname was "The Tiny Avenger."

Dr. James Adcock, a faculty member, often said, "Yeah, we've got to reel her in once in a while, but she knows what she's doing."

The education I received from the University of New Haven was phenomenal. Every time I see Dr. Lee, founder of the Henry C. Lee Institute of Forensic Science at University of New Haven, he asks, "How's Molly's family?"

The faculty cared deeply about these cases, and many of them assisted me with Molly's. I was selected to participate in a pilot group of graduate students who, under the supervision and direction of a faculty member, would evaluate cold cases from across the United States for various law enforcement agencies. The faculty member assigned to supervise us was Dr. James Adcock, whom I married in 2009. I was a perky, twenty-something ingénue, enamored with a sophisticated mentor.

I graduated from the University of New Haven in 2007, and Jim and I did not begin our relationship until well after any conflicts of interest were negated. He is a lovely, brilliant, generous, kind man. While we divorced in 2013, we remain good friends, and coauthored two books, numerous articles, and continue to operate The Center for the Resolution of Unresolved Crimes together.

With the support of my family, Molly's family, and the wonderful faculty and friends at the University of New Haven, I dug in. In Christmas 2006, one of my dearest friends, Megan, painted the dragonfly on the next page for me. Fourteen years later, I now have a fair share of dragonflies from students, friends, and Molly's family.

Residing in New Haven gave me a huge advantage over living in Alexandria. Instead of nearly seven hours away, Molly's territory and answers were now a mere hour and a half from my doorstep. At the time, I saw this as a huge advantage. In hindsight, I wish I had seen it for what it was—a huge risk. The Tiny Avenger was about to get a healthy dose of reality.

Figure 17: Painted by Megan Browne-Dull, 2006.

CHAPTER FIVE

Trash grabs

In cold cases, ironically enough, time is one's best friend. I say this from a behavioral perspective: loves get extinguished, friendships languish, partners in crime morph into enemies. This is one advantage of time, and sometimes the only advantage an investigator has. As those relationships evolve, motivations and loyalties also shift.

For example, what was once only a whisper of suspicion on the part of a lover becomes deafening when the relationship ends. When the noise becomes overwhelming, a former lover, friend, or colleague will reach out to voice their concerns and suddenly a cold case once again ignites, the spark of a fresh lead tantalizing, invigorating.

This is precisely how I came to know of the man in the trailer park. He was one of my first legitimate persons of interest in Molly's case, but to protect the integrity of the investigation, the identity of the person of interest and witnesses who were brave enough to come forward will not be identified.

[JOURNAL ENTRY]

10/27/05 9:29 A.M.

Well, registering on John Douglas's site definitely paid off, I'll tell you that! This morning I received a private message from a user named ▆▆▆▆▆▆. The user stated she was living in ▆▆▆▆▆▆ and that she fled from a dangerous man and that Molly was killed shortly thereafter. She was one of several women involved with this man who were forced to flee for fear of their safety. She claims this man is identical to the sketch done by Jeanne Boylan. She told me she does not believe this is the first murder this man has committed. At the time of Molly's murder, he was in Massachusetts for a jazz festival.

Noted here is the sketch of the man in the white car first composed by law enforcement. It was a start, but Molly's family felt it was a bit too generic, so they engaged the services of Jeanne Boylan, a world-renowned forensic artist who has assisted in dozens of high-profile investigations. Her book, "Portraits of Guilt," features many of these cases.

Figure 18: Police handout of suspect sketch.

Two portraits Boylan rendered were those of Polly Klaas's abductor and the Unabomber. Rather unusual, her technique is highly effective.

Magi recounted her experience with Ms. Boylan to me. They spent several days hunkered down in Ms. Boylan's hotel room. Magi was somewhat surprised when Ms. Boylan did not immediately question her about Molly's alleged abductor. Rather, they chitchatted and during natural breaks in conversation, a question regarding the stranger in the white car would emerge. At the end of the grueling session, below was the result.

Figure 19: The publicly distributed sketch of Molly Bish's alleged abductor by forensic artist Jeanne Boylan.

The plethora of detail and nuance contained in Boylan's image is lacking from the composite constructed by law enforcement. The most important aspect of this rendering is the behavioral information that Ms. Boylan seamlessly conveyed. The perpetrator's persona was slick, dangerous, arrogant, and confident. He held absolutely no concern for the wreckage he would ultimately inflict.

Another feature Boylan captured that's equally important was Magi's description of the way the man held his cigarette—low and with perfectly straight fingers, perhaps a bit more effeminate in nature, and certainly not a common style for male smokers; also behaviorally relevant. While both sketches remain in circulation, the second sketch by Ms. Boylan is generally accepted as a more accurate rendering.

My tipster emailed me a photograph of the person of interest.

[JOURNAL ENTRY]

10/31/05

Nose consistent

Eyes consistent

Age at time of Molly's abduction: 45

Mustache / Hair style consistent

Weight inconsistent: witness states weight would fluctuate significantly based on the level alcohol consumption

Wrinkles in forehead consistent

Cocky expression

I first spoke with my tipster on Halloween, 2005. She originally contacted the Warren Police Department about the person of interest, unaware that the investigation had come under the purview of Worcester County MSP detective unit and their district attorney. Warren officers allegedly informed MSP that there was no reason to contact the reporting witness or suspect although this man matched the sketch, was in the area around the time Molly disappeared, had access to a white car, had a criminal history of abusing women, as well as substance and alcohol abuse. Although he was a con artist with a fascination for blonde teenagers, local authorities allegedly felt there was no reason to pass this information on to the district attorney.

[JOURNAL ENTRY]

11/5/2005

"I need you. You're my everything." –John Bish to me after another consultant had become incapable of continuing due to issues with alcohol, and I was told to stay away from this person.

I feel so alone. I'm lonely. I wonder so often why I have been put in the middle of all this. When I left that note on Molly's website, I never expected to hear back, let alone become involved, uproot my life, and move to Connecticut to help John and Magi. I keep wondering; what is behind my passion? What are my motives? I cannot find any.

Everyone seems to have an agenda. Is there something I'm missing? Is there something wrong with me simply because I want to find out who did this to Moll? I don't want the "glory," I don't want money. I want to be able to know that John and Magi can sleep at night knowing this man can never harm another child again. It is so strange for me. I mourn a girl I never knew...I cry tears for her, I hold Magi as she cries, I hold John. How do I hold myself? How do I reconcile such an illogical grief? Why can I not be like my friends, my peers? Why do I have such an unwavering devotion? I feel my heart break. I keep feeling like I'm not doing enough, not trying hard enough.

We had just learned about trash grabs, a technique used by law enforcement to glean information about their persons of interest. When an individual abandons his or her property for removal, such as putting out trash beyond the curtilage of the home, it is officially abandoned and anyone can legally go through it. So, I thought I'd try my hand at it.

When I pulled into the trailer park where this suspect lived, I was somewhat disappointed. This might be the guy who committed one of the most infamous crimes in Massachusetts, maybe the country. My maternal grandfather in Texas recently told me, "Darlin', if you go lookin' for trash, that's exactly what you're gonna find."

He was certainly right in this instance.

I was freezing. It was about 2 a.m. in the dead of winter, and there I was sitting in my silver Beetle, which I had turned off to avoid detection. Wrapped in a comforter, I watched the trailer from behind binoculars. The trash was out, and all that stood between me and it was a few rows of trailer homes.

I snuck out of my car, teeth chattering partly from the cold and partly from fear, and started tiptoeing across the small patches of lawn between trailers. As I approached the suspect's trailer, an inside light went on. He was reportedly extremely paranoid and kept odd hours. I could hear my heart beating in my chest as I grabbed two huge bags of garbage and ran like hell back to my car.

John Bish had instructed me to call him as soon as I had the trash. As I headed out of the trailer park, my hands shaking, I dialed his cell. "You hot shit! Yeah!" he exclaimed, and I could hear him clap his hands in the background.

I was ecstatic. I did it! "Wanna go get a coffee?" John asked.

"John, it's three in the morning, I'm going to bed" I replied.

"Good job, kid. Good job," John said.

I could hear the smile in his voice.

I drove two hours home and went through the suspect's garbage just as the sun was coming up. Prescription information, bank names, online activity, credit card numbers, and cigarette butts for DNA. Not bad for my first time out.

This suspect claimed to be a prophet; he was extremely religious, and his favorite movie was reportedly Stigmata. Around Christmas that year, I discovered a message written on the lifeguard chair at Comins Pond. In hindsight, I'm almost positive it was written by a disgruntled teenager in the throes of adolescent rebellion. Yet at the time, the message piqued my interest given the location and mention of religion. Additionally, having seen handwriting samples from the suspect, the writing style was similar, as was the inability to spell.

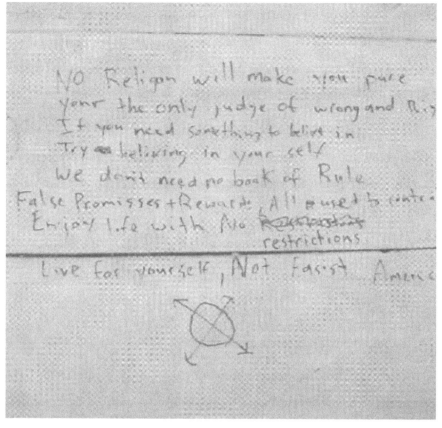

Figure 20: Message on lifeguard chair, 2005.

During the winter of 2005, I also wrote to Nancy Grace to try to get Molly's family on the show. I begged the show producers to be gentle, to not do anything to antagonize or hurt Molly's family. This is how the show began on January 2, 2006.

[SHOW TRANSCRIPT]

> Nancy Grace: Our culture calls it "sweet 16," that time in your life when you have the world by the tail, your whole life before you. Molly Bish's parents dropped their 16-year-old girl off at her life-

guard job on a summer afternoon. They watched her. She walked away. Then they never saw Molly again. Three years later, Molly Bish comes home, bone by bone, 26 bones in all, no clues, no answers, five long years of pain. Good evening, everybody. I`m Nancy Grace. I want to thank you for being with us tonight. Tonight, the ongoing mystery of 16-year-old Molly Bish, a wonderful young girl, so full of life, a Massachusetts lifeguard seemingly vanishes until Molly is found, bone by bone, 26 bones in total. Who murdered Molly Bish?[15]

Bone by bone? I was livid as I watched Magi come apart during the introduction, the expressions on the rest of the family's faces. The media using the unimaginable pain suffered by a family for the purposes of ratings and sensationalism is a pet peeve.

Then, there was the rock. Our witnesses identified this boulder as a place where our suspect would sit for hours at a time, and allegedly claimed something was buried under it. Dr. Adcock and I excavated what had to be an 800-pound rock. By the time we got under the boulder, we were filthy, drenched in sweat, and hoping like hell we'd find something of value.

Bones. I saw bones.

Jim and I looked at each other. It was a heavy moment. As fast as we could document the bones, we dashed back to the university where we waited with bated breath for the results. Were we dealing with a second victim?

No. They were racoon bones.

Figure 21: 800-pound boulder

On June 27, 2006, I decided to surveil our suspect. I wanted to see if he went anywhere; with any luck, it would be the pond. It is common for certain typologies of offenders to revisit crime scenes to relive the thrill of committing the crime. I sat in my silver Beetle in the trailer park, watching from a safe distance with binoculars. I could see his front door perfectly.

He finally emerged around 9:30 a.m. Just as his front door closed, my cell rang. It was my mom. "What's wrong?" she asked.

"What? Nothing's wrong," I answered, while trying to keep an eye on my guy. He had walked out of my range of vision.

"No, something's wrong. I can feel it!" she insisted on the other end of the line.

I looked up. In my rearview mirror, I saw the suspect sitting right behind me in his car, watching me. "I'm fine, I promise. Gotta go! Love you!" I said, cranking my engine and flooring the gas.

He was right on my tail, a foot off my bumper. I had to get on the highway where I could lose him. He followed me up the on-ramp. I didn't know what else to do, so I jerked my wheel hard to the right and slammed on the brakes. He sped by me and didn't come back.

I sat on the side of the road, shaking and sweating. That was it for me. I asked John if I could take everything to the Massachusetts State Police. He approved, warning me to, "Keep my head low and my ass to the wall." At the time, I didn't understand what he meant. I do now.

I went to see the Massachusetts State Police. My upper lip was sweating profusely. My hands, slick with sweat, clasped the report I had carefully prepared. My heart was pounding and I felt as though I might faint. This was my entrée, I thought. This is the beginning of my professional life. You've got to nail this, come on, get it together!

"Ms. Stein?"

I remember the gleaming oak table the most. I remember their faces reflected in the perfectly polished surface. Captain Thomas Greene sat at the head of the table surrounded by what seemed like his entire staff. Greene's face had a reserved smile, not unlike the expression a cat has before it pounces on a mouse.

Introductions were made, and they asked me to show them what I had. I was nervous of the authority, and so focused on presenting my material in a professional, coherent way, that my presentation felt almost dreamlike. Afterwards, Sergeant Francis Leahy showed me around the office, and I was able to see firsthand the massive effort

WHO TOOK MOLLY BISH?

they had put into Molly's investigation thus far. Sergeant Leahy then asked me, "Have you ever read 'The Blooding'?"

I had not.

"I'll send you a copy. You might find it interesting," he grinned, clapping me on the shoulder.

Then it was over. In looking back on that first meeting, I wonder what their agenda was, and what they thought mine was. Did they think I wanted to be a trooper? Did they mean to intimidate? Were they just trying to get a read on me?

My only agenda in that meeting was to get through it without fainting or vomiting. Beyond that, it was only to get answers for Molly, the only thing I've ever wanted.

I called John. I had survived meeting the Massachusetts State Police, and it went well. Or so I thought. Shortly after that meeting, John and I went to an event for the newly elected Worcester County district attorney Joe Early.

John slapped Early on the back, grinning from ear to ear as he introduced me. "Watch out for this one, she's going to do your job better than you!"

Sergeant Leahy did send me, "The Blooding." I've always wondered if there was a reason for it.

CHAPTER SIX

The politics of murder

[JOURNAL ENTRY]

11/1/06

Further Cowardice: The Massachusetts State Police. Dr. Adcock and I were at Anna Maria College yesterday so he could give a lecture on death investigations for first responders.

A captain with the Massachusetts State Police called the Chair of the Criminal Justice Department at AMC and protested, saying Dr. Adcock has no business lecturing at the college and he shouldn't be teaching police officers how to be investigators, that it was their job and their job only to investigate crime.

Of course, a certain trooper from the Worcester County State Police Detective Unit continues to take great pleasure in antagonizing me over the phone, telling me, "You don't know shit about this case; the only shit you know is what you read in the newspaper."

I don't understand it; they put out a reward, advertise for information, yet when they get it, they reject it outright or belittle the source because it didn't originate from the high and mighty CPAC unit. They knew about the person of interest since August 2000, and never called the tipster back.

They knew about the person of interest in 2006 and never called that tipster back.

I am so tired. I cannot help but feel exhausted and frustrated. I'm trying to do good, have integrity, and help a family and Molly. I don't want money, I don't want recognition; I want John, Magi, Heather, John Jr., and Mikaela to be able to sleep at night knowing that the son of a bitch who did this to Molly will never hurt another child.

Those experiences were my first introduction to what I now refer to as the politics of murder. When I said that I had no idea what I was getting into, that was an understatement. I had no knowledge of the deeply rooted political machine that ran the Massachusetts State Police, and the district attorney offices of the Commonwealth of Massachusetts.

Massachusetts is unique—only four cities investigate murders that occur within their jurisdiction: Boston, Springfield, Worcester, and Pittsfield. All others rely on the Massachusetts State Police, the agency awarded The Golden Padlock. The agency my own husband worked for; the agency that allegedly accused an innocent man of running Molly Bish over with a sand truck, and threatened many others, including me.

Their intimidation, while it caused a degree of anxiety, was not a deterrent to me. I felt it was machismo compensation for what certain individuals may have lacked in actual investigative ability.

Shortly after Early was elected to the Worcester DA's office, Jim and I were at John and Magi's house one evening when reps from MSP's Worcester unit delivered a victimology form from the FBI to the family. "They thought it'd be a good idea," the trooper mumbled.

Jim and I looked at each other. Victimology is the cornerstone of any investigation. If you know your victim, you will know your perpetrator. If you don't know your victim, you have nothing. You don't know why this person may have been targeted, who their enemies may have been, and what type of predator they may attract.

Why did the MSP deliver a victimology form to the family years after their daughter had been abducted and murdered? Why weren't these questions asked the very first day Molly disappeared? We were baffled. If these questions had been asked, Molly's investigation may not have languished in the manner it did.

The next suspect who came to my attention I nicknamed The Walrus, due to his handlebar mustache. He was a cunning man and certainly gave off significant red flags. At the American Academy of Forensic Sciences meeting in 2007, I presented my report on this man to Richard Walter. When Richard told me to run, not walk, to the district attorney's office with the information, I damn well listened.

A current or prior law enforcement official being involved in Molly's case was a possibility, as the location of her remains was on the border of three counties. Some believed that a suspect with a law enforcement background would know that such a confusing jurisdiction is advantageous, making apprehension more difficult.

[JOURNAL ENTRY]

12/27/06 11:30 P.M.

Okee dokee. NEW person of interest popped up on Justice-4-Molly's MySpace page. His screen name is Walrus627. He is retired from the Department of Corrections in Massachusetts. He sent me the following message on MySpace on 12/27/06:

"Hi,

I am retired from the Commonwealth of Mass. dept. of corrections. I live a few towns away from the town Molly grew up in I guess? I have followed the case as I'm sure many people have from this area. What's interesting for me is she was abducted on my birthday June 27th. I honestly can say I have felt real feelings for the Bish family. I think most parents do. God I just cannot fathom there (sic) pains and pray I never do. But I am a civic minded man and am wondering what if at all could I do to help?"

This suspect described his interests as fishing, camping, hiking, target-shooting, and hunting. He had thirty friends on MySpace, the majority of whom were blonde women. We began conversing on MySpace. Walrus627 represents my suspect.

[MYSPACE CONVERSATION]

Walrus627: I was pleasantly surprised by your photo

Me: Really?

Walrus627: Yes what a pretty woman you are wow marry me – Sarah I know beauty when I see it

Me: So you're a blond guy huh? My hair goes really blond in the summer

Walrus627: oh yeah – you seem like such a sweety pie

Me: thanks, lol, you don't know me too well though, haha, nah, just kidding

Walrus627: I have done a lot in my life to help others, still do, very active

Me: Obviously; you care about Molly enough to try and help her...that is so kind

Walrus627: I have been to a few things about her, the ride, donating money

Me: Wow, cool

Walrus627: I have a button with her photo

Me: Me too, I wear it all the time

Walrus627: do you know that my birthday is the date Molly was abducted?

Me: I read that in your email...wow, there's a twist of fate, huh?

Walrus627: June 27, yes

Walrus627: I want to ask 1?

Me: Sure

Walrus627: Have you ever dated an older guy?

A friend helped me create a false profile on MySpace. She then corresponded with the suspect while I corresponded with him at the same time so he wouldn't suspect it was me. In a conversation with my friend, Walrus627 relayed that he prefers blond women, wouldn't mind if the girl was seventeen, and that he wanted to meet at a state park to act out a rape fantasy.

Richard Walter emailed me on March 24, 2007, reiterating the need for me to run, not walk to the prosecutor's office. So I called the Massachusetts State Police.

[JOURNAL ENTRY]

4/12/07

I spoke with Sergeant Francis Leahy of the CPAC Unit in Auburn today, and we've scheduled a meeting regarding my person of interest next Friday, 4/20/07 at 09:30 hrs at the Auburn barracks. I haven't told John about the meeting yet, he was reticent to do it and wanted me to send him everything. When I considered further, I decided not to send John the material; there are conversations I feel he shouldn't read, that would upset him immensely.

In conversations with Walrus627, he would suggest ways Molly and her killer could have met, what could have happened to her, and it was extremely graphic. I couldn't bear the thought of John Bish seeing that, and was afraid of what he might do if he did. I was trying to protect him and get my information into the hands of the only people who had the power to take the matter further, even if my faith in them wasn't particularly strong.

When I met Walrus627 for coffee at a crowded Dunkin Donuts to talk in person, I was hoping to obtain his DNA from a coffee cup to give to the MSP. When our conversation finished, Walrus627 took his cup with him. Maybe he still had some coffee left, I thought, dismayed. But when he got into his car, he looked over his shoulder at me, shot a wicked smile, winked, and tossed the empty cup over his shoulder before driving off.

I met with the Massachusetts State Police on April 20, 2007. However, that decision caused my first rift with the Bish family.

[JOURNAL ENTRY]

5/13/07 7:03 P.M.

We had our meeting with the State Police, and now John Bish has betrayed me. Last week he called Dr. Harper at the Institute complaining about my "reckless" behavior by going to the MSP. I can't believe he would do this to me; for the last four years I have done nothing but devote my time and effort to resolving Molly's case. Granted, my efforts, my time, it was my choice to give both freely without the expectation of anything in return. However, anything I did was with the best of intentions.

I would NEVER do anything to hurt Molly's family deliberately; how could I? They are a part of me. They took me under their wings four years ago; they gave me love and guidance and support. Sure, there were times when John and I got angry at each other or disagreed, but we were always able to right our wrongs, start fresh again, and move on. I can't believe this. I was trying to protect him from emotional pain for God's sake!

At the time, I couldn't understand what was happening. For a couple of months, John had begun acting erratically, and it led to a rift. John is one of the gentlest souls I've ever met. Yet, during that time he was often angry. The littlest thing set him off, and he was complaining of severe headaches. In hindsight, I recognize that these were warning signs of something worse to come, but at the time, I felt only guilt and overwhelming sadness. I thought I was doing the right thing by going to the MSP just as Richard Walter recommended, and felt betrayed. So, I backed off. I sent an email to the MSP saying I would no longer be looking into Molly's case.

[JOURNAL ENTRY]

5/13/2007

Dear Sergeant Leahy,

I wanted to inform you I will no longer be actively pursuing and or investigating Molly's case. I have also informed John Bish of this via email. I do, however, want to set the record straight for my own peace of mind and reputation.

I did not fully comprehend how upset John was when I came to see you on April 20. This whole matter started because I would not send John my packet of information regarding Mr. ████████. I had previously informed him that I was looking into Mr. ████████ as a possible person of interest. However, for the reasons you outlined at our meeting (the family is put on an emotional roller coaster every time they are presented with another possible person of interest), I was reticent to show John the material I presented to you (i.e. the instant messenger conversations, etc.) as I thought they would be emotionally upsetting to him. I can understand him wanting to see the information but I didn't think it was appropriate and wanted to give it over to you so it could be properly investigated. At any rate, I apologize for any trouble I may have caused you or Molly's family; I had and still have the best of intentions and it has been a pleasure working with you. If anything further comes to my attention regarding Molly's case I will pass it on immediately.

Very Truly Yours,

Sarah Stein

I received a response from Leahy two weeks later.

[EMAIL FROM SARGEANT LEAHY]

05/31/2007

Dear Sarah,

Good morning. I was surprised to receive your letter earlier today, but I must truthfully tell you, I was relieved. The decision you have made to back off of this investigation is the proper one. While I understand, as you stated, that you were well intentioned, I feel your actions were inappropriate for a civilian with no formal police training and acting with no supervision.

I can tell by the tone of your letter than you are hurt by some event that has happened, but I'll give you an example of your not understanding the dynamics of this case. When you state, "...it has been a pleasure working with you," I have to set the record straight; we have never worked together.

If you wish to work on major investigations, I suggest you do what we in this Office have all done: score high on a police entrance exam; graduate an academy; pay dues on the road and show some raw investigative talent; interview for a detective position; be accepted into a detective unit and investigate those cases which a supervisor assigns.

Sincerely,

Francis D. Leahy
Sergeant, #1342
Mass State Police

[JOURNAL ENTRY]

5/31/2007

This is truly hilarious; I had sent the email to Leahy hoping he would merely accept my resignation for what it was, accept it, say thank you, let it go, and move on. The comment "it's been a pleasure working with you" was meant as nothing but a professional courtesy. How insecure must one be to be threatened enough by the earnest efforts of a twenty-four-year-old girl, to distort a comment made in the context of a professional courtesy into a crass and demeaning remark regarding my intelligence?

I have learned so much from this experience. The bitter taste I expected to linger has become surprisingly sweet. The skin in which I live, that I expected to flake, come away like moistened paper and dissolve, has hardened and endured, reminding me of the unexpected pleasure that comes when you realize you still have the ability to surprise yourself.

I have learned that no matter the magnitude of the injustices one suffers, no matter the depth of the lashes ignorant people may inflict upon your heart and spirit, there is one that has suffered more: the victim for whom you are the voice. Though this experience has tainted my faith in law enforcement, brought many tears upon my face, and wrenched my spirits to all imaginable depths, I am alive, and I will persist.

Molly Bish was a child of innocence; her only future on June 27, 2000 was the afternoon. Her dreams at 16 were to find true love, save her money from her summer jobs to buy a Jetta and go on a cross-country historical road trip with her Poppy, go to college, become a teacher like her mother, and raise a family of her own.

In moments, her future, the unfolding of her dreams, were stolen on that fateful summer day. Where seconds before she lay basking in the warmth of the summer sun, her breaths of innocence quickly faded. This man, this murderer, snatched the foundation of a family from beneath them, all with forethought and calculation.

In the brief respite between the assault and death, I wonder what Molly thought. What were her last words? Whatever they were, they were inconsequential to her killer. He murdered her still and dumped her like refuse on a wooded hillside to be picked apart by animals and swallowed into the earth.

There will be a thousand Mollys during the course of my career. Yet there was only one dragonfly circling my cap at graduation, and I think of Moll. Though I never met her, I know her; I know that her voice will always remain alive in my heart. Here on earth, she wanted to lay in the sun and protect children. I'm sure she is doing so in her heaven. I hope she knows I will do my best to mirror her desire to protect others in this mortal life, that I will never give up, and that I will love her always.

Magi Bish called on Wednesday, June 20, saying John suffered a massive hemorrhagic stroke.[16] I went to the ICU in Worcester. When I arrived, Magi fell apart in my arms. This could not come at a worse time—the vigil was the following week, as was the ride.

Magi explained that for the past month or so, John was behaving irrationally and suffering from terrible headaches. On Friday night, they were supposed to go to dinner, and John kept saying he needed to rest. So Magi went to check emails and then heard John calling for her. She ran upstairs and found him lying on the floor vomiting blood.

Magi called 911 and John was first transported to Harrington Hospital where tests showed bleeding in his brain. He was then life flighted to UMass Memorial Hospital where the family was given the option to let John go or gamble and do survival surgery; they chose the latter. As of now, the doctors couldn't give a definitive prognosis.

[JOURNAL ENTRY]

6/27/2007 10:01 A.M.

I arrived at Comins Pond at 0930 hours. There are no signs of activity and it is very calm. It is very hot and humid out with a mild breeze. There are a ton of dragonflies around. John's condition is improving. The smell of the water and the summer air is lovely here; a small slice of paradise turned sour. I know Molly's watching over John.

On November 2, 2007, a benefit was held at the Sturbridge Host Hotel & Conference Center, A Night to Honor John and Magi Bish.[17] The event was to raise funds to help with John's care and make the family residence handicap accessible. Multiple companies pitched in to help the Bish family at no cost. Kady Builders from Brookfield built the family a front porch, Palmer Paving paved their driveway, and the entire community came together to lift the family up.

I attended the benefit and watched John and Magi, surrounded by friends and family, dance to "Stand by Me." The fact that John could walk, let alone dance, was beautiful. The fact that I was there to witness it gave me the strength I needed to walk away, and finish the education I needed to return one day to give Molly and many others the justice they all deserved.

While it was a bittersweet goodbye, I knew in my heart it was not a permanent one.

[JOURNAL ENTRY]

8/2/2007 2204 hours

"When are you coming home?"
"Well honey, I am home...I'm back in Connecticut now."
"No, I mean home home...here."
Mikaela's plaintive voice resonated in my ear when I called this
evening, tugging at my heart. She just turned eight. Today is
Molly's twenty-fourth birthday. John is still in the hospital. God
willing, everything will work out well.

Mikaela is Molly's niece, and Heather's only child. I met her in 2004, when she was almost five. I had met Molly's family for dinner at Olive Garden. Mikaela's cat had unfortunately just been run over by a car. At dinner, she was sitting next to me scribbling a picture.

"What are you drawing, honey?"

"My kitty—she's in heaven with Auntie Molly now."

I will never forget those words, how my heart ached when she said them. A silent tear slid down my cheek and I quickly wiped it away before she could see.

I watched Mikaela grow up. When she was little, she loved egg whites and hated the yolks. She loved to paint John's toenails when he was asleep. When she was a teenager, she was a lifeguard at Comins Pond. It felt like I didn't take a single breath that summer. When she graduated high school, she got a dragonfly tattoo. I wrote the following letter to her on her graduation.

[LETTER TO MIKAELA]

June 10, 2017

Dearest Mikaela,

I simply cannot believe that I am sitting here writing to you on your graduation. The fourteen years that I have known you have simply flown by. I remember the very first time I met you. You, your mom, and John and Magi and I went out to dinner at Olive Garden. You were drawing a picture of your little kitty that had unfortunately just passed away. When I asked you where your kitty was you said, "now she's in heaven with Auntie Molly."

I remember how much my heart ached for you and your family that day, and how in that moment I promised myself that I would do whatever I could to help look after you and protect you. Turns out...you didn't need any help at all! ☺

I am so amazed and inspired by the young woman that you have become: selfless, fearless, brilliant, beautiful, and so kind. You already possess all the attributes you will ever need in this world to succeed. I feel so blessed to have shared some of your life's journey thus far and hope we will continue to remain connected for many, many more years. I can't wait to see what your future hold for you.

Please always remember to keep your joyful, playful spirit, don't ever let anyone ever tell you you're not enough, and never compromise your integrity for anyone or anything. Spread your beautiful dragonfly wings and soar into the world, knowing that you have so many people who love you and will always love you and be here for you no matter what.

I love you so much and am so proud of you.

All my love,

Sarah L. Stein

CHAPTER SEVEN

Piled higher and deeper

After sitting through a miserable training for the Child Abduction Response Team delivered by a fellow PhD, I now understand why cops may be leery of those with doctorates. This guy was arrogant, belittling, and a horrible speaker. When I lecture to law enforcement today, I always begin by saying, "Look, PhD just stands for piled higher and deeper. You are the ones doing the hard work, I'm just here to help give you some tools."

I began my doctoral studies in the fall of 2009, at The University of Southern Mississippi, a world away from Warren, from Molly. I was asked to consider the program by a faculty member from the school at the Academy of Criminal Justice Sciences annual meeting the year prior. After completing my master's, I discovered that I was either under or overqualified for every job that appealed to me. When Jim and I married in 2009, we had agreed that a PhD was my best option.

The day before classes started, I went to introduce myself to my professors. Dr. Lisa Nored, who chaired the criminal justice program, called later that day to offer me an assistantship. I had no clue what that was. "Well, basically, we pay your tuition, give you a stipend, and you do twenty hours of research or teaching a week," she stated.

The next day at orientation I met a woman who would become one of my best friends, Dr. Vanessa Woodward-Griffin. My mother, having grown up in Texas, had given me a beautiful white lace parasol from Italy, to shield my face from the sun. Vanessa and I hadn't yet formally met but she looked in my direction, rolled her eyes and laughed, saying, "You've got to be frickin' kidding me."

I knew immediately we'd be friends.

Vanessa and I would get together in the evenings, have cocktails, and finish our work. There were many late nights when we said our goodbyes over a shot of NyQuil, sleep a couple hours, and show up at the university by 8 a.m. to start all over again. My goal was to finish my doctorate before age thirty.

In 2010, I presented a paper at the International Crime, Media & Popular Culture Studies conference entitled, "Strain, Shame, and the Shadow: A Study of Deviancy Among Celebrities." I didn't know it in 2010, but I was predicting my own future. Following was the abstract.

[ABSTRACT]

This paper presents an analysis of the deviant behaviors committed by four celebrities: Tiger Woods, Michael Vick, Britney Spears, and Lindsay Lohan. The personal histories, careers, and deviancy of each celebrity are examined regarding the causal

WHO TOOK MOLLY BISH?

factors of the deviant acts, the nature of the acts, and the public response to the deviance.

General Strain Theory by Agnew (2006), the theory of the shadow put forth by Jung (1959) and the concepts of reintegrative shaming and disintegrative stigmatization by Braithwaite (1989) are used to outline why celebrities indulge in deviancy and whether or not the celebrity can be reintegrated positively into social culture.

Four hypotheses are addressed in this paper. The first is that celebrities are held to such a high standard of scrutiny in the public eye, they are unable to express their shadow conventionally. As such, the strain of maintaining a perfect image becomes unbearable and they resort to deviancy.

Secondly, it is expected that deviancy will follow a particularly successful period in the celebrity's life. It is also discussed whether there is a difference in the nature of deviancy due to gender. The author believes that males will be more likely to externalize strain with violent and/or sexual deviancy, while females will be more likely to internalize strain via eating disorders and/or drug and/or alcohol abuse.

Finally, it is expected that the nature of shaming a celebrity is subjected to (reintegrative shaming versus disintegrative stigmatization) will be correlated with whether or not deviancy persists or ceases.

I took my comprehensive exams in my last semester. Exams consisted of three twelve-hour days and covered six areas of expertise including administration, research methods, statistics, theory, your cognate, and law. Each examinee must answer two of the three questions provided. I passed, writing over 150 pages in three days.

Next came the dissertation, inspired from the material I learned at USM, my Jung-filled childhood, and, of course, Molly. I titled my dissertation, "The Cultural Complex of Innocence: An Examination of Media and Social Construction of Missing White Woman Syndrome." I merged the criminological and Jungian worlds to construct my theoretical framework. Jung posited that all cultures have complexes that arise from the collective unconscious. I believed that as a western, primarily Christian society, we have been unconsciously conditioned to view the blonde-haired, blue-eyed Caucasian female as an archetypal image of innocence through advertising (alluring vs. innocent blondes), art, music, film, photos, and religion.

The term Missing White Woman Syndrome is thought to be attributed to Professor Sheri Parks from the University of Maryland,[18] and alleges that missing white women, particularly attractive ones, will receive disproportionate media coverage when compared to their racial counterparts.

My research took this a step further. From my observations with Molly's case, I believe that because society has been unconsciously conditioned to identify blondes as innocent, this element would also play a role in how a missing person is portrayed by the media, received by the public, and further, the investment of law enforcement in relation to the investigation. My findings supported these hypotheses.

I examined 533 missing person cases selected at random from The Charley Project, a comprehensive website that features a plethora of missing person cases. I studied groups of blonde-haired, blue-eyed

Caucasian females, other Caucasian females with varying hair and eye colors, and other races of female victims. I examined all media associated with each of the cases and found that blonde victims were seven times as likely to be referred to as innocent by the media, more likely to have quotes from law enforcement regarding the status of the investigation, and had a higher average of news coverage.[19]

While completing my dissertation, I was also teaching criminal justice and forensic science at Clayton State University about twenty minutes outside Atlanta. Months later, as I drove to Mississippi to defend my doctoral dissertation, the final step towards a Ph.D., I got caught in the worst thunderstorm I had ever been through. I kept thinking that I had better not die before I get this damn degree.

After presenting my dissertation defense, I was asked to wait in the hallway while the committee of professors discussed the merits of my research and whether to award me a Ph.D. After waiting about ten minutes, Dr. Nored emerged. "Dr. Stein? We're ready for you."

I did it. I had passed and was now Dr. Sarah L. Stein. My knees almost gave way. At age twenty-nine, I had met my goal. As soon as I finished defending, I jumped in my car, and drove back to Georgia.

Clayton State was a great university when I was there, and my students were phenomenal. An urban university, it was gritty and real. I had to earn these kids' trust, and I did.

A few years ago, a student sent me the following picture, saying, "Remember the good old days?"

Figure 22: Dr. Stein staging in a tree for her students' mock crime scene.

Those *were* the good old days. I enjoyed setting up mock crime scenes for students to process. I can't remember what made me laugh, but the photo above is one of the few in this field where I'm smiling.

Around 2012, my marriage to Jim was ending and I was looking for jobs elsewhere. A teaching job had opened at a university in western Massachusetts. I applied and got an interview.

I researched who was on the search committee and noticed two were retired from the Massachusetts State Police. One was Dr. Denise Kindschi Gosselin, chair of the department I was applying to, and John "Jack" Drawec, Esq. who ran the forensic science program. Though I was already thinking it, my parents cautioned me, "Don't say anything about Molly Bish on that interview!"

The search committee took me to lunch at the campus dining room. Jack and I were alone at the table while everyone else were getting their meals. "So, you work on cold cases, huh?" he smiled.

I nodded.

"You ever hear of Molly Bish?"

I choked on my salad, composed myself and said, "Vaguely."

I got the job.

Six months later, Jack and I had become friends and colleagues. I was teaching the laboratory portion of his Introduction to Forensic Science course when I confided about Molly. He told me why he asked me about her the day we met. He had transferred to the crime scene unit of the Massachusetts State Police just days before she disappeared. Her investigation was his first one in that assignment. The universe works in strange ways.

After I returned to Massachusetts in 2013, I learned that John and Magi had stepped back from their role in the Molly Bish Foundation. John's health remained fragile and they were both simply exhausted. Heather, Molly's sister, had taken up much of the work and was spearheading investigation efforts. I wrote a letter and gave it to her at Molly's vigil in 2013, asking if it was alright if I work on Molly's case again. She agreed. I felt redeemed, vowing anew to find Molly's killer.

At that same vigil I saw Sergeant Leahy, whose only comment to me was, "You look good."

"Yeah, thanks." I'm sure you're thrilled I'm back, I thought.

After Heather and I reconnected in 2013, one person we naturally circled back to for elimination was Rodney Stanger, the suspect who Mr. Shamshak, the investigator out of Boston, discovered in 2008, and now in prison for murdering his girlfriend. After some initial research into Stanger, I discovered his home address in Southbridge was a mere few blocks from where Molly had taken her lifeguarding lessons. I immediately sent this to the Massachusetts State Police. By this time, Sergeant Leahy had been promoted to captain.

[EMAIL]

10/13/2013

Hi Captain Leahy,

Sorry to bother you again; was going through some old journals today and came across an interview where I had noted that Molly took her lifeguarding lessons at the YMCA in Southbridge? I'm sure you all have looked at this, but I just thought it was interesting that it's located at 43 Everett Street, only 0.3 miles from Stanger's old residence....don't know if it's relevant, just thought I'd pass it along.

Captain Leahy responded, acknowledging receipt of the information, copying Worcester DA's Joe Quinlan, who was handling Molly's case, as well as Shawn Murphy, one of the trooper's assigned to Molly's investigation. I decided this was worth pursuing. With Heather's blessing and on my own dime, I flew to Florida to interview Stanger at Union Correctional Institute.

[JOURNAL ENTRY]

9/10/2014

- Make Stanger Binder
- Flight Reservations:
  - ○ Outbound:
    - Southwest Airlines #333 – BDL to BWI 9/18/2014 0610 hours
    - Southwest Airlines #4966 – BWI to JAX 9/18/2014 0840 hours
  - ○ Return:
    - Southwest Airlines #1131 JAX to BWI 9/18/2014 1920 hours
    - Southwest Airlines #1178 BWI to BDL 9/18/2014 2155 hours
- Union Correctional Institution: Raiford Prison, 7819 NW 228th Street, Raiford, FL 32026

Following was the interview plan I wrote and memorized before my departure.

[INTERVIEW PLAN]

Mr. Stanger, it's a pleasure to meet you. My name's Sarah – did anyone tell you why I'm here with you today? I'm here to help you – to give you the chance to tell your side of a story – and only you have the power to do that Mr. Stanger. I am not a police officer, you are under no obligation to speak to me. I'm someone who works on cold cases – for the past eleven years I've been looking into Molly's case. Is it ok if I tell you a little bit about myself before we get started? I want to tell you about the first man I ever spoke with in a situation like this (remember: use minimizing language). May I show you his picture? (Show him Weaver's photo). His name is Ward Weaver. When he was nine years old, his father abducted, sexually assaulted, and murdered a young woman. He made Ward help him bury her body...when he was only nine – completely helpless.

Then, Ward went into the military – and he went to Vietnam. He saw horrible, horrible things – things that scared him very badly. A few years later, Ward made two poor choices (show him the photos of Ashley and Miranda). Unfortunately, it was found that these girls were buried on Ward's property. Ward would describe that when he did these things, he would zone out – he knew what he was doing and that it was a mistake, but he just couldn't help it because he wanted to be loved. I believe, through being with these beautiful girls, Ward thought he could reclaim that innocence that had been stolen from him by his father, and then obliterated when he went to Vietnam. He just wanted to be loved, to be innocent, and he made a mistake.

The reason I'm telling you this story, Mr. Stanger, is that I believe Ward was not alone in how he was feeling. I'm telling you this Mr. Stanger, because even though we have just met, I believe your pain, your trauma, is in a way like Ward's.

I understand you experienced things that were very traumatic for you when you were young – that you too were in Vietnam and betrayed by your own family – those very people who should have been there to protect you. Then, you were betrayed by Chrystal. I cannot imagine what you experienced.

You know the other thing I didn't tell you about Ward's story is that everyone, of course, was focused on the girls as victims, but they had both been flirtatious with him – they had even fooled around – but the first girl, right in the middle of making out with him, she changed and flipped on him – and he got scared (flip the tables, empathize with his view of himself as a victim). I mean, you guys are always getting the shit end of the stick – a girl flirts with you, leads you on, then changes her mind and you get punished? Bullshit.

Anyway, the District Attorney and the media tried to make him out to be a monster, but he wasn't – that's another reason I think you can relate to this story, Mr. Stanger – everyone is focusing on someone else being a victim, when it's you who has been victimized by the police, the people trying to get you in Massachusetts, and the media.

The reason I'm here today Mr. Stanger, is to first make sure you know you're not alone. Your story is unique, and you are a smart, capable man. Ward wasn't nearly as smart at you – he made the mistake of putting the bodies in the yard, and he interjected himself into the investigation.

The other reason I'm here today Mr. Stanger, is to help you tell your story. I know you are not the monster everyone is making you out to be. I know you yourself are a victim – but I also know you are a real man and that you alone have the power here; you've always had it. I know you have a story that no one has heard, and I am hoping you will choose to tell me that story. Shamshak called you a sociopath on live television. I'm not out to get you, Mr. Stanger. I'd be just as happy to rule you out as a person of interest and sit here and talk with you. I know that if Shamshak or the Massachusetts State Police find something first that can link you to Molly, they will make you out to be a monster – I want to give you the chance to tell me you're not.

On September 18, 2014, I arrived at Jacksonville International Airport. I went to pick up my rental car and was given a minivan.

Totally appropriate to roll up to a prison with authority to interview a potential murderer. Wonderful.

All along the drive, I enjoyed the warm Florida sunshine, watched dragonflies dance around the minivan, and repeated my speech to Stanger over and over in my head.

I hate prisons. Not that anyone particularly cares for them, but for me, it's claustrophobic. I arrived, walked through a metal detector, signed in, and spoke with assistant warden Steve Rossiter.

We walked through a series of metal doors: the kind where each one is closed and bolted shut with a jarring buzz before the next door opens. I could feel my throat getting tighter and tighter as we walked. It was for Molly. Repeat, it was for Molly.

[JOURNAL ENTRY]

9/18/2014

Raiford, Florida
Union Correctional Institution
Arrival: 1245 hours
Stanger doesn't want to talk
1405 hours: Assistant Warden Rossiter delivered my letter to Stanger. Stanger took it but hadn't read it when Mr. Rossiter walked past five minutes later. Mr. Rossiter indicated the sergeant on Stanger's cell block would call him in a bit to update him on whether Stanger read the letter.

Stanger refused to see me. Epic failure.

[JOURNAL ENTRY]

9/18/2014

JAX International Airport

So, I feel like an epic failure after today. I know I shouldn't but having to tell Heather he refused to talk fucking broke my heart. I have to keep reminding myself that this is progress in a way, it's just very slow.

A little more than a month after my visit to Stanger, the following headline appeared on Boston 25: "Molly Bish, Rodney Stanger May Have Crossed Paths."[20]

Where did that leak come from? Certainly not from us. Heather and I were growing more reticent to provide the Massachusetts State Police with information.

In 2014, Jack Drawec and I became involved. We had become each other's best friend, haven, and partner. That same year, Heather invited me to Missing Children's Day at the State House in Boston. In 1983, May 25, was deemed as Missing Children's Day by President Reagan. The Department of Justice holds a ceremony each year to recognize individuals and organizations for their efforts to help missing children.

It was May 25, 1979, when six-year-old Etan Patz disappeared on his way to school in New York. It was the first time he was ever allowed to walk to the school bus alone. He was the first missing child on a milk carton.

Molly's family had spearheaded the ceremony in Massachusetts, and would recognize those individuals whom they felt contributed the most significantly to fighting the epidemic of missing children. I asked Jack if he would come with me.

The tradition was to take a private bus donated by Lizak's from Warren to Boston. That day, we loaded up the bus with masses of yellow roses for Molly. The driver got lost on the way to the State House. Jack went to the front of the bus and guided the driver. We barely made it.

I remember the weight of the bouquets as I carried them in heels from the bus up the steps to the State House, and into the rotunda. Huffing and puffing, we took our seats as the ceremony began.

I looked down at the program for the first time and saw my name listed as one of the award recipients that year. I grabbed Jack's arm and pointed. He smiled and kissed me on the forehead. Magi squeezed my arm, "It was Heather's idea," she whispered.

I didn't understand why I was receiving this; I hadn't yet done anything. I was humbled, and more determined than ever to find Molly's killer.

At the beginning of our relationship, Jack told me he and his uncle Bill go on an annual photography trip. Jack's photos are stunning, and he uses them to create calendars for friends and family. He often says, "I take pictures of beautiful things because I took too many pictures of things I couldn't bear to see," referring to his crime scenes photos.

In June 2014, Jack and Bill took their photography trip to Oregon. While he was away, I had an idea. I wondered if anyone had searched the opposite side of the road from where Molly's remains were found for additional evidence, like maybe a weapon or her clothes such as the pink tank-top and flannel boxer shorts.

Figure 23: Bacon Road as seen from Google Earth.

Bacon Road is unpaved except for the portion that leads to the Nenameseck Sportsmen's Club, which was used as headquarters during the search for Molly's remains. The club's rifle range is visible in the bottom of the photograph above. Beyond that small road is a yellow gate that blocks further access. Bacon road, however, was still accessible by vehicle, and would have been a logical, undetectable escape route for the killer. On the other end of Bacon Road is Route 32, a major roadway that runs through several towns. Molly's killer would not have been noticed.

On June 15, 2014, I went out to Bacon Road. I had my backpack and tucked inside the top pocket was the yellow ribbon John Bish had given me that first day at Comins Pond.

I had my case notebook, plastic bags, paper bags, gloves, a ruler, and various other tools. It was a beautiful summer day. I had been out to Whiskey Hill many times alone and wasn't concerned, nor was I expecting to find anything. The troopers responsible for recovering Molly's remains were so thorough, they even recovered her tongue ring. What in the world was I going to find that they hadn't?

About half a mile down, I looked to my left and saw a large clearing with an odd tree. The temperature dropped and I immediately got goosebumps from head to toe. I felt something I couldn't explain. I immediately got on my hands and knees and began to sweep away layers of dead leaves and dirt. That's when I saw the tip of a black plastic trash bag.

I put on gloves and photographed a small portion of the bag that was visible. I dug more. The bag was old; so old, in fact, that it had split open. I began to sweat and could feel my heart pounding in my chest. Shaking, I sat down in the dirt. With the deafening silence of the woods closing in, the warm summer day suddenly seemed surreal. Buried in that old black bag was a pair of boxer shorts and remnants of pink fabric—the same color as Molly's tank top.

Figure 24: Evidence Dr. Stein collected from Bacon Road on June 15, 2014.

I texted Jack the photos I took. He was at Hood River in Oregon, taking much more pleasant pictures. "What do I do?" I asked.

"Call the MSP right the fuck now."

I didn't call, yet did send the following email to Trooper Shawn Murphy of the Worcester unit.

[EMAIL]

June 15, 2014 3:43 P.M.

Hello Trooper Murphy,

I'm so sorry to bother you especially on a Sunday but would you please give me a call at your earliest convenience? I found some items on Bacon Road off the trail near Nenameseck that may be consistent with the boxer shorts Molly was wearing.

Thank You,
Sarah

Trooper Murphy called, advising he was at another scene and asked me to wait for him. When he arrived at approximately 8:30 p.m., I took him to the location and watched as he stood over the site.

He was quiet, head bowed, and the weight of the moment was not lost on him. I gave him the items and while we sat in his cruiser, I noticed a Promise Molly button he kept in his cruiser. I felt then that he cared, and that I had done the right thing by turning over what I had found.

Figure 25: Trooper Shawn Murphy on June 15, 2014, 8:50 p.m.

The MSP didn't tell Molly's family about the discovery or show them photos of what I had found, so the decision was made to give the story to Kathy Curran, a longtime advocate of the Bish family and reporter with WCVB Television.[21]

Molly's family, from my perspective, was furious with authorities. The story was aired prior to the annual vigil on June 27, 2014. That year was the first time the district attorney or representative from his office was not present at the vigil.

Former Colonel Reed Hillman of the MSP was the emcee for the event. Noting district attorney Joe Early's absence, Hillman asked Jack where they were.

"Not my turn to fucking watch them," Jack replied.

That was the turning point. We began to question the integrity of MSP's investigation into Molly's murder. Over the remainder of the summer, Heather and I discussed various ideas for how to reignite interest and generate fresh leads in the case. With the family's blessing, I created a flyer to post at restaurants, sportsmen's clubs, bars, and other gathering establishments.

Then, one night as I laid in bed, in that beautiful space between consciousness and sleep, another idea came.

Figure 27: A cross for Molly.

Figure 26: Dr. Sarah Stein with John & Magi Bish.

Figure 28: Dr. Sarah Stein contemplating the case.

CHAPTER EIGHT

Just one piece

The first district attorney to handle Molly's investigation was a man by the name of John Conte. He was known for frequently using the phrase that investigators were "just one piece" of information away from solving Molly's case.[22]

During the late summer and early fall of 2014, I had an idea. It occurred to me that perhaps we could use Dr. Robert Keppel's research which indicated that in ninety-five percent of cold cases, the perpetrator's name can be found in the case file. While I didn't have access to Molly's case, I did have access to public information, and the public was just as hungry for answers as we were.

I pitched the idea to Heather: let's get a hotel to donate a room, do a one-day event, advertise the hell out of it in the press, and ask people, specifically those with knowledge and/or tips from the first thirty days after Molly's disappearance, to come forward and tell their story again, or for the very first time.

Heather loved it.

We stressed in the press releases that no law enforcement would be present at the event. It would be run by me with assistance from my students.

My logic behind having no law enforcement at the event was that people are intimidated by their presence. In Molly's investigation, MSP had accused some individuals of involvement in the crime when they had none. I wanted people to feel as comfortable as possible when telling any sensitive secrets they might have been keeping for fourteen years, using the calm environment of a hotel, not cold, sterile police barracks.

I bought snacks and bottled water and put them on each table in the conference room. We had some music playing in the background. Overall, it was a peaceful environment. Following were the instructions I gave to the volunteers:

[CAMPAIGN TEAM BISH]

"Just One Piece"

VOLUNTEER INSTRUCTIONS:

Thank you so much for donating your time today to help with the "Just One Piece Molly Bish Tip Campaign." We hope that this event will give us the one piece of information we need to bring Molly's abductor and murderer to justice. Before you begin taking information from the public, there are just a few things I'd like to review with you:

Allow the witness/tipster to fill out the form on their own unless they ask for assistance

Be encouraging to the witness/tipster. Do not ask questions such as "Why did you wait so long to come forward?" Instead, say complimentary things such as "Thank you so much for coming forward," and "We are so grateful for your help."

Make sure that both you and the witness/tipster sign the statement form

Make sure that the witness/tipster's handwriting is legible

Before allowing the witness/tipster to leave, read their entire statement back to them (beginning with their contact information) to ensure that everything is correct.

Thank the witness/tipster again before they leave and assure them that they will be contacted personally by Dr. Stein as their lead is investigated, give them Dr. Stein's business card, and encourage them to reach out if they think of anything further.

After the witness/tipster leaves the room, give the statement form to Dr. Stein

Thank you again! Do not hesitate to ask if you have any questions!

Sarah Stein, PhD

The Sturbridge Host Hotel & Conference Center kindly donated a conference room. The press releases were put out about two, then one week in advance.

On the day of the event, October 11, 2014, as we walked into the hotel, Magi lamented to me, "I think I know why they donated the room. Molly had applied to be a lifeguard at the hotel but they turned her down because she didn't have enough experience."

We had an overwhelming outpouring of support from the community, and the tips poured in throughout the day.

I believe that Molly and a higher power were in that conference room that day. The first call I got came on October 8, three days before the event, and the last two tipsters came from the event on October 11. All three tipsters identified a person of interest who was previously unknown to law enforcement—Mr. Smith—the man whom I believe abducted and murdered Molly.

At 8 p.m. that evening, we shut down our operation. My students who helped that day, Brandi, Carole, Joseph, Tyler, Julianna, Tara, Rachel, Ariana, Matt, Samantha, Alex, Heather, and Daniel, I couldn't thank enough for what they did. Their courage may very well have helped to find a killer.

Molly's family headed home, the media packed up their gear, and I gingerly took down the photos of Molly taped to the walls of the conference room. I hope I did you proud, I thought as I returned the pages to my binder.

On the drive home, I kept my window down and my heater cranked. The chilly evening air of New England in October smelled of crackling smoke from campfires, fresh, alive.

Jack and I reflected on the day. Two themes emerged from all the individuals who came forth with information:

- They had called the MSP with their information before but never received a call back.
- They were too afraid to talk to the MSP.

My mind spun. They hadn't been called back; they were all too afraid. What was wrong with this system? Enraged, I didn't sleep at all that night.

The next morning, I reviewed notes regarding my new person of interest, Mr. Smith, and prepared to dig in, again.

Jack and I met with Molly's family to review the tips we collected from the event. Heather was adamantly against sending information regarding Smith to the state police. I was equally concerned.

Jack and I did a little digging. We thoroughly re-interviewed the witnesses who came forward. They alleged that Smith was staying at Old Sawmill Campground in West Brookfield. The campground is no longer operational, but Smith's father owned a camper and the family was well known there.

The witnesses stated that Smith had been absent from the campground from the morning of June 27, 2000, until the following morning, June 28. They said that his father's girlfriend, while at the campground's pool that day on June 27, was asking where her vehicle was. It was a white, boxy-shaped car.

The morning of June 28, Smith returned to the campground with the white vehicle, now severely damaged and muddy. Allegedly, at 7:30 a.m., Smith stated to one individual, "You've got to stay here with me, you've got to say you saw me. I was in the woods all night, something really bad happened."

Smith's knuckles were allegedly bloodied and he had scratches on his face. He then allegedly took a bottle of peppermint schnapps, one of his favorites, invited people to do shots with him, drank the entire bottle, and passed out for the remainder of the day.

In the days following Molly's abduction, Smith was reportedly seen at approximately 3:30 to 4 a.m. getting rid of several items in the campground dumpster. In addition, the damage done to the vehicle had apparently rendered it inoperable. Allegedly, Smith asked the campground owner for assistance. The owner of the property reportedly told him, "Just put it over there," pointing to a pile of various types of refuse such as refrigerators and mattresses.

The witnesses also claimed that Smith began bragging that he was a person of interest, that he had been interviewed by the MSP, and that he had been cleared when others at the campground began to notice his resemblance to the composite sketch. One person went so far as to put a copy of the wanted poster on the door of Smith's camper. He allegedly said to a witness, smiling, "So you think it was me, huh?" and walked away.

We interviewed his ex-wives. There were several. All of them reported two important details:

- He was an alcoholic.

- He disappeared every year during the last week in June until July 4, and then returned, as it was a significant holiday to him.

These women had no idea where he went, only that he would go on benders. One ex-wife was a woman who was native to Africa. When I called, her English was very broken, but she had an extreme reaction when I mentioned Smith. "Very bad man! Very bad man! Tried to strangle me! I run!" and she hung up the phone.

Another ex-wife has permanent hearing loss from the beatings he gave her, and a third suspected Smith had been unfaithful because, according to her, "He gave me the crabs."

We then found another witness who had spent time with Smith shortly before Molly disappeared, and was told they had frequented Comins Pond together. I decided to test this individual a little further. "How exactly do you know that it was Comins Pond?"

The new witness described it perfectly, right down to the little bridge one must cross to get to the beach. So now, we knew that Smith was familiar with the pond, had access to a white vehicle, and had been gone from June 27 and June 28, and allegedly returned with bloodied knuckles, a scratched face, and a wrecked white car. He was also desperate for people to say they saw him, desperate for an alibi.

This was looking stronger and stronger. Jack and I finally decided it was time to face him.

On October 25, 2014, Jack and I went to Smith's apartment.

[CASE NOTES]

S. Stein

October 25, 2014

On October 25, 2014, John Drawec and I interviewed one Mr. Smith, a person of interest in the abduction and murder of Molly Bish, at his residence, located at ▓▓▓▓▓▓▓ from 1200 – 1315 hours.

Mr. Smith allowed us entry into his home. His apartment is a one bedroom and smelled heavily of cigarette smoke. There were two packs of Maverick Menthol cigarettes on the living room table.

Mr. Smith asked us if we wanted to sit down. I explained to him why we were there and asked him if he had ever heard of Molly's case. He replied that he had seen something about it on the news.

We then asked Mr. Smith if there was any reason his name would come up in the investigation and he said that his parents stayed at a campground in West Brookfield; at that point I casually asked if he had ever been to Howard's Drive-In during that timeframe to which he replied that he frequented the restaurant (we did not tell him we knew Molly worked there).

Mr. Smith stated that no one had ever questioned him in Molly's abduction and murder prior to this date and denied being told by several acquaintances and relatives that he resembled the sketch of the gentleman seen at Comins Pond. Mr. Smith appeared to slip and said, "Oh, the mother saw this guy talking to her?"

We then asked Mr. Smith about his personal background. He claimed he had only started drinking when the economy "tanked" and that he has been sober for three years. Mr. Smith additionally accused his ex-wife of being the true alcoholic and that she enjoyed coffee brandy and schnapps, which is what his relatives said that Mr. Smith would drink. Mr. Smith adamantly maintained that he was never violent while drinking and he would "never go after a girl who didn't want him; there are plenty of women out there." Mr. Smith then continued that he would never "intentionally" hurt anyone, and appeared to be considering his options, nodding his head when I suggested the possibility that whoever took Molly may not have intended to hurt her but that it was an accident.

Mr. Drawec then stated that we were there to give him comfort, peace of mind, and interview him without law enforcement in his own home, and that it was his chance to tell his side of the story. I followed with the fact that we had several witnesses placing him at the campsite bloodied, disheveled, and under the influence of alcohol following Molly's disappearance; he did not outwardly deny these allegations.

Mr. Smith asked when Molly had been found and I stated that the police were only able to recover partial remains; Mr. Smith appeared relieved. I followed up with the assertion that Molly's bathing suit is at the crime lab and they are going to try new testing techniques for DNA (I wanted to see what kind of response this would elicit) – Mr. Smith became very nervous. Mr. Smith then looked at Mr. Drawec and asked, "So what's your deal?" Mr. Drawec responded by stating that he was an attorney who assisted families with these types of cases. Mr. Smith then asked, "When they come for me, will you represent me?" Mr. Drawec replied to Mr. Smith, indicating that would be a conflict of interest. Mr. Smith shrugged his shoulders and said, "Ok." I then asked Mr. Smith if it was alright if I had a cigarette (I had gone out and purchased a pack of Marlboro Lights – my former brand, to see if I could observe him smoking). Mr. Smith replied, "Sure!" and grabbed a cigarette for himself as well: he held the cigarette with straight fingers and held it low. As soon as Mr. Smith observed me and Mr. Drawec looking at his hands, he immediately curled his fingers and said, "Uh, yeah, it's real hard for me to keep my fingers straight 'cause I was in an accident, see?" He just happened to have a photograph of his hand from this "accident" on his coffee table which he proceeded to show us.

Mr. Smith also stated that he had never been to Warren but then stated he had been there to visit his son; Mr. Smith contradicted himself many times during the course of the interview; he also admitted he owned a white Buick LeSabre but claims it was stolen following Molly's disappearance. We then asked Mr. Smith about hunting and fishing and he said that he was an avid bass fisherman (Comins Pond has bass), and that he also fished at Comet Pond in Hubbardston. Mr. Smith also stated he was a member of the American Legion in West Brookfield and then switched to the one in Worcester.

In parting I told Mr. Smith that our job was to follow every lead and that thus far in the investigation we were not able to discount him as a person of interest. I told Mr. Smith we would continue to pursue this until we were confident he was not involved in Molly's abduction and murder. He said "there are bad people out there and I want to help you" – Mr. Smith stated he would call me when he tracked down his employment records from 2000. However, we had already spoken to his previous employers and confirmed he was unemployed during this time. I asked Mr. Smith as we were walking out the door, "so you really had no idea why we were coming today?" He smiled at me and said, "no, my son told me."

Behavioral Indicators:

1. When he first opened the door, Mr. Smith appeared as if he knew why we were there, which he later confirmed when he said his son had "given him the head's up" about out visit, yet he denied knowing anything about Molly or why we were there to begin with

2. Mr. Smith would not look Mr. Drawec in the eyes

3. Mr. Smith appeared to become more comfortable when we suggested that Molly's murder was not planned and that it was an accident

4. Mr. Smith appeared nervous as the prospect of DNA testing

5. Mr. Smith admitted he frequented Howard's Drive-In

6. Mr. Smith did not deny that he had been seen bloodied and disheveled at the campground following Molly's disappearance

7. Denied ever being violent while drinking

8. Had a white Buick LeSabre

9. Claimed he had never been to Warren but then retracted and stated he had when his son worked for a company there

10. Has an affinity for bass fishing (Comins Pond has bass)

11. When Mr. Smith smoked in the apartment, he held the cigarette in a manner consistent with the sketch done by Jeanne Boylan

Below are Jack's notes from the interview with Smith.

[CASE NOTES]

10/25/14

West Brookfield – Old Sawmill Campground

Parents – Both passed away

2000 – worked as CDL driver

Construction companies

Buick LeSabre registered to him?

American Legion Worcester

Maverick Menthol cigarettes held as in original sketch

Says he gets drunk and goes to sleep

July 4 – Fireworks and drinking

Advised as to witness statements

Wht. Car stolen?

Hunted Petersham area – Sketchy

Bass fishing enthusiast – Comins Pond

Quaboag Lake

Comet Pond Hubbardston

Fished w/son or whoever around

Denied spousal abuse

Says wife was alcoholic

Denied ever getting violent

Would travel to do automotive repairs on his own when not working usually at people's houses

White car – Admitted

Ever told you look like the sketch – denied

Ever tell people you were questioned but cleared – denied

Denied knowing Molly

    Admitted going to Howard's regularly

    Admitted going to the campground regularly

Son worked in Warren

Ever black out? No

Did state police come to you yet? No

Did district attorneys come to you yet? No

Contradicted on Warren presence

Disorderly arrest while drunk called cop an asshole

Class B CDL license

At end, he asks me, "what's your deal?"

Atty firm has represented families of missing victims

"When they come for me, will you represent me?"

Ah, no! That would be a conflict

Figure 29: Make and model of 1986 white Buick LeSabre.

After we left the interview, Jack stated that while he was still not completely positive Smith was the killer, he was sure Smith was the man in the white car at the pond that day.

In our follow-up to this interview, I called the Worcester Police Department. They confirmed that Smith had reported two vehicles stolen, but neither was a white Buick LeSabre. Lie number one.

One of Smith's former employers to whom we had spoken called me in the days following our interview. He said Smith had called the office, sounded extremely intoxicated, and asked for his employment history, which the employer had already given us, showing that Smith was not employed during the time Molly was abducted.

Smith then left me a voicemail, stating that he called his former employer, and that they didn't keep records from that long ago. Lie number two.

A friend of Smith's on Facebook called me and said that Smith had messaged her instead of his brother in Florida, whom he meant to message. Smith allegedly said he had to get out of Massachusetts, and was going to be arrested for Molly Bish's murder.

Jack and I apprised Molly's family of the situation. Jack was adamant we get the information to the MSP. Heather and I were reluctant; we felt that they would not conduct a proper follow-up, ignore us completely, or mess it up.

Jack then had the idea to bypass the MSP completely, and directly contact Joe Quinlan in the district attorney's office, therefore backing the Worcester unit into a corner, forcing them to investigate.

Joe Quinlan, unfortunately now deceased, was a wonderful man of integrity, and certainly stuck his neck out for Jack and me. He was a lion among men, and a dogged prosecutor. While working as a prosecutor, one night after hours, Joe came face to face with an MSP commander, catching him during the commission of a crime. The commander attacked Joe with a knife. It took over 300 stitches to sew up Joe's wounds.[23]

Molly's family and I agreed. If we were going to send this to anyone, it was going to be Joe Quinlan. Jack composed and sent the following email.

[EMAIL]

10/30/2014

Joe,

This is Jack Drawec. Don't know if you remember me. I ran the MSP Crime Scene Services section out of Agawam a while back and retired as a DLt from the MSP in 2009. I am presently running a forensic science program at a university. I hope you are doing well.

Part of my representation includes victims' families. My firm represents the family of a missing man (presumed murdered) and I have also been collaborating on the Molly Bish case with her family. You may not realize this, but Molly was my first homicide case in CSSS, as she went missing a few days after I was transferred into the section. Our office was called in to assist CSSS-Devens in the days after she went missing and also when her remains were located. To this day, the case is dear to my heart, especially when I meet with the Bish's.

You may have heard that the family launched a "Just One Piece" campaign a few weeks ago. The campaign was initiated to get that "one piece" of evidence that your office has constantly reminded the public that was needed to solve the case. I assisted with the campaign along with Dr. Sarah Stein, a colleague who ran the operation. Several of our students assisted with gathering the tips that came in.

Before the campaign started, Dr. Stein received information on a suspect through a telephone call. On the day of the campaign, others (not related to the first) mentioned the same name. I assisted Dr. Stein in following up on some information, including meeting with the suspect. (Something I advised her not to do alone.) Attached is a summary report that Dr. Stein prepared for the family based on this suspect.

113

You may ask why this is only being brought forth now. During the campaign, we received information from several tipsters that they were intimidated as to how some people were treated by investigators in the initial investigation. Some related that "witnesses" were being treated as criminals. Others stated that they called the State Police and never received a call back. Others relating to this suspect were told by the campground owners not to get involved.

You may be aware that Dr. Stein has given CPAC information in the past and some received very little if absolutely no follow up. As such, she (and Molly's family) has been a little leery as to how Molly's case is presently being handled by the DA's office and the MSP assigned there. I have assured Dr. Stein and Molly's family that you would read her report and make sure this is investigated by your office. Other than Whitey Bulger and the Boston bombing, this case has utilized more Commonwealth resources than any other and I would be remised if your office isn't looking to close this out. This may be our chance.

Joe, I met this guy myself and something is up with him. He lied and was very evasive when speaking about this case. Please take the time to review this matter carefully.

I am leaving for a forensic science conference in Hershey, PA tomorrow afternoon, but wanted you to have this information personally ASAP. I will not be back till Thursday (11/6) evening. I will have my cell phone with me. Please feel free to contact me ANYTIME should you need anything further. Again, I have assured the family that it is important to get this information to your office for review. They do expect some sort of follow-up.

Joe, on a side note, it has been disturbing to me as a former MSP officer to learn that victims' families often time think of themselves as being victimized by the investigators and the system as investigations continue. The family in one of my other cases related that it would simply be nice for investigators to check in every now and then, especially on important anniversaries (such as the day their loved one went missing) and let them know that they are still working for them. It was not unnoticed that DA Early did not attend the vigil held for Molly in June. According to Molly's family, it was the first time that the DA was not represented at that event since Molly went missing. Even former MSP Colonel Hillman commented directly to me that it was upsetting as he was the emcee for the vigil and the DA was on the agenda to speak. I really think that someone, maybe from victim/witness, should remember these families and let them know that the DA's office is constantly working for them.

In closing, please let me know whether the information is helpful or not. I know that any disclosure would need to be held in strict confidence. Let's hope that this helps your office in giving Molly and her family some peace.

My best regards and wishes,

Jack

Game On.

Figure 30: Pink fabric Dr. Stein found on Bacon Road.

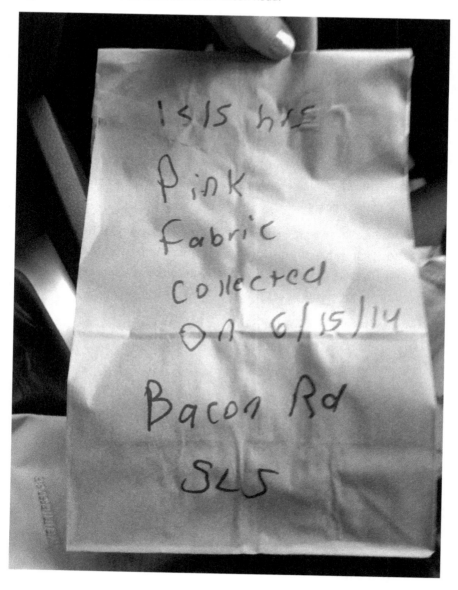

CHAPTER NINE

Just one car

Jack's letter to Assistant DA Quinlan was the political equivalent of detonating a ton of explosives within the seemingly impenetrable bureaucratic walls of the Massachusetts State Police.

Jack and I were told the unit commander of Worcester forwarded Jack's email to the unit commander of Hampden, which had, for a time, overseen Holly's Piirainen's murder investigation. Both commanders reportedly laughed at Jack's allegations of incompetence, coercive behavior, and insensitivity to families' pain.

Nonetheless, Jack's letter forced the Worcester unit to investigate Smith. They were unable to eliminate him, which led to a meeting between Molly's family, Terry McLaughlin of the Worcester DA's office, Trooper Shawn Murphy and Lieutenant Philip Dowd of the Worcester detective unit, Jack, and myself.

We met at the Brookfield Court House. Once again, I found my upper lip sweating through my makeup, not from fear this time, but anger. I had played by their rules and given them credible information. I provided the lead about Stanger that someone leaked to the press, turned over the clothing I found, and with the bravery of Molly's community, may have very well found Molly's killer. And they still wanted to meet and play this game of politico?

I had daggers in my eyes as we walked into that room. Protective of Molly's family, I was ready to tear ass if the opposing team made any shady moves. Terry McLaughlin had pudgy fingers and the handshake of a dead fish. He had sweat around his collar. Apparently, I wasn't the only one keyed up.

They couldn't deny that Smith was a viable person of interest and couldn't be ruled out. Trooper Murphy, whom I had faith in only months before, and judging from the Promise Molly button he kept in his cruiser, felt he had truly cared about Molly, turned to me and Jack and said, "Well, we don't even know how qualified these two are to investigate a homicide."

Jack's face flushed. I bit my lip hard. In hindsight, I have little doubt that Trooper Murphy was instructed by the district attorney's staff to denigrate us.

Lieutenant Dowd of the Worcester unit used to work for Jack, and knew Jack had been involved in over 250 death investigations and testified on multiple high-profile homicides.

Jack's final MSP assignment was working in internal affairs. He was so trustworthy he was given the responsibility to investigate his own colleagues. In each interview, the accused was represented by counsel. A couple years ago, a scandal rocked the Massachusetts State Police. Troopers were accused of putting in for overtime they never worked. Days into the scandal, Jack received a call from a former MSP colleague, a command staff member. The colleague recalled that Jack had investigated something similar years before, and the colleague under investigation suddenly retired before he could be disciplined.

"Hey Jack, you remember so and so? Yeah, if they had let you lock him up, this shit wouldn't have happened."

"I know," Jack replied.

For my part, I had consulted for multiple police departments, taught cold case investigations at the Dutch Police Academy, and created accurate victimology and suspectologies for child abductions. As a professor, I was trained by the best forensic minds in the country, had personally presented at over fifteen conferences across the nation, published two books and numerous articles on cold case investigation, all while consulting for families including Molly's. I'm not saying Jack and I are better than anyone else, but we are damn well qualified to conduct an interview of a homicide suspect.

The meeting concluded with the Worcester office promising they would investigate. Once in the hallway and Molly's family was out of earshot, one of them whispered to Jack, "We know he's lying."

What was the point of the theatrical bullshit? To dress us down, or dress themselves up for not finding the son of a bitch sooner? An

WHO TOOK MOLLY BISH?

attempt to regain power and credibility? I think Jack would have kicked their ass right then and there if I had let him.

For the simple reason that Molly's family needed the correct spelling of his last name, Jack got advance notice that he was an award recipient at Missing Children's Day, 2015. I was so thrilled, and so proud of him. I've always told him he should have been colonel of the Massachusetts State Police. His reply is always the same—he didn't have the political juice, nor would he have wanted the position. Being qualified and having a strong moral code isn't enough. You need politics to succeed in law enforcement. I resent it.

The morning of Missing Children's Day was unseasonably warm for New England. The bus traditionally used to make the trek—a plush, air-conditioned vehicle with its own bathroom—was out of commission. Instead, that morning we would be taking a school bus.

Jack had brought his father, Bill, with him to the event. They were both dressed appropriately in suits. Poor Bill, at age seventy-six, grinned, not minding the news of no air conditioning or cushy seats. His son was being recognized for contributing to the fight for resolution for a family of a murdered child. He was so proud.

The bus parking lot is across the street from the XTra Mart where Molly and Magi bought water and snacks the morning of her abduction. As we loaded flowers into the bus, one of the volunteers with the Molly Bish Foundation was driving into the parking lot. Out of the corner of my eye, I saw another car come out of nowhere from the opposite direction and T-bone the volunteer's car.

Glass and metal smashing, scraping, and wrenching broke the otherwise peaceful, if somber, morning. As Magi and I stood in the bus watching the wreckage, she began to shake and sob. I took her arms in my hands and looked into her eyes, trying to get her to focus. "Magi, it's not Molly. It's not her; she's safe, you're safe. Everything's okay...breathe....breathe..."

The primal terror in her eyes was horrific. I could see her trauma, her anguish, her unrestrained panic. I grabbed her close and held her in a bear hug until she stopped shaking. The volunteer was fine, thank God, and we got on our way.

It was actually a really nice ride into Boston. The summer breeze was flowing through the open windows of the bus and we took backroads to the Massachusetts Turnpike.

After the event, Jack asked if I would take a picture of him and his father Bill in front of the firefighter's memorial. Jack's father was a retired volunteer fire chief, and one of the

Figure 31: Jack Drawec with his father Bill, 2015.

sweetest men I ever knew. After Jack and I began dating, I learned of the beautiful marriage that Jack's parents shared. High school sweethearts, they were in love for all the years they spent together.

For significant events such as birthdays and anniversaries, Bill had flowers put at their church in Carol's memory. One year he gave me her flowers. It was such a poignant moment that signified love, acceptance, and trust.

There is such a haunting element to the Missing Children's Day ceremony at the State House. It's an almost surreal experience. Sarah McLachlan's song, "In the Arms of An Angel," is traditionally played while a slideshow of missing and murdered children fills the grand rotunda. There is reverent silence.

The ceremony concludes with the reading of names of missing and murdered children in the Commonwealth of Massachusetts. A bell echoes between each name, and members of the audience come to the front to collect a flower for each missing or murdered child.

Sadly, family members of many victims either cannot make it to the event or are deceased themselves. That day, Jack and I collected flowers on behalf of children who had no one in the audience to claim them. Jack was then called to receive his award, a humbling moment for him.

Both of us are eternally grateful for having been given those awards, though we didn't feel we deserved them. There hadn't been an arrest, there hadn't been a conviction. What, really, had we done?

Figure 32: Jack Drawec & John Bish, 2015.

After the ceremony, the group went to lunch at a local seafood place, spreading out all over the restaurant and circulating from table, chatting, laughing, and sharing clams, sandwiches and sodas.

At the same time we were enjoying lunch, the future Secretary for the Executive Office of Public Safety & Security, Dan Bennett, who was serving as Worcester County's first assistant district attorney at the time, was escorting Joe Quinlan down the hall at the State House. As the two emerged from the dimly lit hallways into the blinding sun, Bennett turned to Quinlan and allegedly said, "Oh, by the way, you're no longer doing homicides."

Joe Quinlan was also honored that day by the Bish family for his commitment to help resolve cases like Molly's. The only man we had trusted with our information and who had enough integrity to hold the feet of the Worcester unit to the fire was now gone.

When we learned of this development, Jack, Heather, the rest of Molly's family, and I were beside ourselves. What now? What the hell are we going to do now?

I called Joe. He said, "I'm sorry Sarah, I can't help you anymore."

Joe did the only thing he could to solidify his reputation as a man of integrity—he separated himself from the Worcester unit and got out of Massachusetts. He didn't push that investigation for me or for Jack—he pushed it for Molly.

Joe moved to New Hampshire and took a prosecutor's job in a remote town and then died.

Joe Quinlan wasn't the only casualty of Molly's case. As time moves forward in any cold case investigation, witnesses and others who are crucial to the investigation will die. That's why it's so critical to get accurate statements as quickly as possible. This was one reason that the investigative grand jury was empaneled by former district attorney John Conte—to get everyone's statements on record.

In Molly's investigation, her former boyfriend, Steven Lukas died in an auto accident.[24] Kenneth Tatro, older brother of Molly's friend Gerard, died. And Peter Rambiszewski, the son of a Massachusetts state trooper, died in an auto accident on June 10, 2003, one day after Molly's remains were identified. Richard Greco, an assistant district attorney strongly associated with Molly's case, died in 2007.[25]

I was fortunate to be able to interview another individual prior to his passing in 2012, John Borowiec, the caretaker of St. Paul's cemetery behind Comins Pond.[26]

Mr. Borowiec pointed me to the spot where he specifically saw the white car parked on the morning of June 27, 2000. It was parked approximately where the patch of sunlight is on the roadway in this photo.

Figure 33: Location where white vehicle was reported to have been parked.

Below is the view we believe Molly had as she was abducted from the beach, was walked down the trail, coming out into the cemetery where the white car was parked.

Figure 34: From Comins Pond to cemetery.

While looking at these images in 2015, another idea came to me. We did a Just One Piece campaign. Why not a Just One Car campaign? We had the VIN number for Smith's vehicle. We knew it had not been reported stolen, that the registration was not renewed, and we knew it had not been officially reported as being salvaged.

I created a flyer for the campaign and developed a comprehensive list of all salvage yards in Massachusetts, Florida, Rhode Island, New York, Connecticut, Vermont, Maine, and Pennsylvania. Fifteen years later, we were on a hunt for the car.

The Sturbridge Host Hotel was kind enough to donate another conference room. I ran the operation with my usual crew of volunteers, including three new additions, Eleni and her mother Ann, dear friends from Massachusetts, and Jenny, a student of mine who has a natural affinity for the field. Eleni was interested in criminal justice, and Ann wanted to help.

Heather was there as well but stayed in the background as she was finishing her doctorate. Following were the instructions I gave to the volunteers:

[CAMPAIGN TEAM BISH]

"Just One Car"

VOLUNTEER INSTRUCTIONS

You will be calling various salvage yards in search of the vehicle pictured above – a white, 1986 Buick LeSabre. Please say the following when calling each establishment:

"Hello, my name is _____. I am calling on behalf of private investigator Dr. Sarah Stein in reference to the unsolved homicide of Molly Bish in Massachusetts. I am attempting to locate a vehicle that belonged to a person of interest in our case. Would you please be able to check if your business has purchased this vehicle from this gentleman since the year 2000?"

Allow them to respond – if they indicate that they do not keep records back that far, ask them if they could please check their more recent records as you have both the VIN and the names of the individuals who might have sold the vehicle.

After completing the search, thank the representative you've been speaking with and let them know if they come across any

additional information to please call Dr. Stein at▓▓▓▓▓▓▓▓▓▓▓
Then record the results of your conversation in the space below
the name of your agency. An example of a call that did not result in
finding the vehicle would be as follows:

> Al's Auto Salvage
> Name Searches: Negative
> VIN Search: Negative

An example of a call that did result in finding the vehicle would be
as follows:

> Al's Auto Salvage:
> Name Searches: Positive (indicate which name)
> VIN Search: Positive

If you happen to be speaking with an individual who reports that
they **DO** have the vehicle we are looking for, or **DID** do business
with one of the above-mentioned individuals, please ask the
representative to hold and give the phone to Dr. Stein
immediately.

Thank you so, so, so much for your help!!! Let's find the car!!! ☺

Around 11 a.m., Eleni started waving her hands frantically in the air. Everyone ended their calls so Eleni could put the man on speaker; he was the owner of a salvage yard in Florida, near an area where our person of interest had family.

"Lemme read that VIN to ya," he drawled.

Yes . . . yes . . . yes, the letters and numbers were matching. Yes, yes, yes . . . . and . . . the last digit was wrong. I could feel the air in the room deflate and watched Heather's eyes sink as she exhaled—she hadn't taken a breath. I was heartbroken.

We didn't find the car that day, but I did get a call from one of the witnesses who had originally named Smith as a person of interest at the Just One Piece campaign. He said the car might be buried at the Old Sawmill Campground.

It rained that year on June 27, the day of Molly's vigil. Her vigil was traditionally held on the Warren town common. The town priest from the church across the street was kind enough to offer their facilities. We all ushered inside as thunder clapped.

I looked down at the program for the vigil; Heather's daughter, Mikaela, was going to sing. Not only was she going to sing, but she was going to sing "If I Die Young," written by Kimberly Perry in 2010.

[LYRICS]

IF I DIE YOUNG, the Band Perry

If I die young
Bury me in satin
Lay me down on a bed of roses
Sink me in the river at dawn
Send me away with the words of a love song
Uh oh uh oh
Lord, make me a rainbow I'll shine down on my mother
She'll know I'm safe with you when she stands under my colors, oh
and
Life ain't always what you think it's gonna be, no
Ain't even gray but she buries her baby
The sharp knife of a short life,
Well I've have just enough time
If I die young

Bury me in satin
Lay me down on a bed of roses
Sink me in the river at dawn
Send me away with the words of a love song
The sharp knife of a short life,
Well I've had just enough time
And I'll be wearing white when I come into your kingdom
I'm as green as the ring on my little cold finger
I've never known the lovin' of a man
But it sure felt nice when he was holding my hand
There's a boy here in town says he'll love me forever
Who could have thought forever could be severed by
The sharp knife of a short life
Well I've had just enough time
So put on your best boys and I'll wear my pearls
What I never did is done
A penny for my thoughts, oh no I'll sell them for a dollar
They're worth so much more after I'm a goner
And maybe then you'll hear the words I been singin'
Funny when you're dead how people start listenin'
If I die young
Bury me in satin
Lay me down on a bed of roses
Sink me in the river at dawn
Send me away with the words of a love song
Uh oh (uh oh)
The ballad of a dove
Go with peace and love
Gather up your tears, keep 'em in your pocket
Save 'em for a time when you're really gonna need 'em oh
The sharp knife of a short life,
Well I've had just enough time
So put on your best boys, and I'll wear my pearls

Mikaela's voice, smooth and graceful, floated through the church as the storm raged outside. Jack put his arm around me as a tear fell from my cheek. Mikaela, sweet Mikaela, whom Molly only got to know a brief time before she was taken. She didn't ask for this life, but she rose to the occasion of honoring her aunt that evening. I thought of the song in the context of Molly's fate. One verse kept playing over and over in my mind:

A penny for my thoughts, oh no I'll sell them for a dollar

They're worth so much more after I'm a goner

And maybe then you'll hear the words I been singin'

Funny when you're dead how people start listenin

How valid this verse was, how applicable and appropriate for Molly, her family, and their legacy.

When John and I had dinner together in D.C., he told me that he had never asked for this life, that if he could go back, he would in a second, but that in between, he was going to fight like hell, because it was a war. It took a sixteen-year-old girl being abducted on her eighth day of a new job to change the way things worked in the Commonwealth of Massachusetts.

Before Molly, there was no AMBER Alert, there was no Missing Children's Day, a single lifeguard was allowed to be alone at a location, and there was no Molly Bish Foundation, or The Molly Bish Center for the Protection of Children & the Elderly. There was also no attention paid to siblings of abducted and murdered children.

In 2004, after I had visited Molly's family, I noted that whenever we were out in public, a number of people would approach John and Magi to extend their sympathies. Molly's siblings, Heather and John Jr., rarely received acknowledgment, let alone the same heartfelt sympathies extended to their parents. During my internship at the National Center for Missing & Exploited Children, I asked what research had been done on the effects of child abduction on their siblings. The answer: none.

In 2007, the U.S. Department of Justice, Office of Justice Programs, Office of Juvenile Justice and Delinquency Prevention published "What About Me? Coping with the Abduction of a Brother or Sister."[27]

Heather Bish and John Bish Jr. were contributors to the project, and I'm so glad they had the opportunity. How agonizing to not only have lost your sister, but then to feel as if you are becoming invisible in her wake, your feelings, your pain seemingly less than that of your parents.

Heather is a force and a rock who will fight her entire life for Molly. John Jr. is a softer soul, and in all my years of knowing him, only spoke of his baby sister a handful of times. When he did, the feeling that his voice evoked in me was not unlike listening to a plaintive, solitary mourning dove. A broken cry; a shattered soul whistling in the winds of the universe.

In July 2015, Jack and I purchased a beautiful post and beam home on eight wooded acres in Ware, Massachusetts. It was secluded, private, beautiful. One of the first things Jack hung in our new home was a dragonfly. The Bish family attended our housewarming. We were toasted into our new home and John Bish sang in Polish. It was a wonderful night, and I loved our home.

Figure 35: Sarah's home.

At the beginning of October 2015, almost exactly one year after we hosted the Just One Piece campaign, the Massachusetts State Police decided they needed to bone up on their investigative skills. A story by reporter Samantha Allen was published in Telegram & Gazette on October 5, 2015.

[NEWS ARTICLE]

State police 'homicide school' aims to sharpen murder investigation skills.

"The weeklong closed program will feature wisdom from experienced investigators and lawyers. Former longtime Worcester County investigator Lt. Daniel Richard and Trooper Keith M. Egan, who works in the Worcester County office, will lead a session on unsolved cases. Other topics include the utilization of social media to solve crimes and investigating the deaths of children."[28]

Troopers Keith Egan and Shawn Murphy worked together on Molly's investigation, as did Lieutenant Daniel Richard. They had questioned mine and Jack's capability and qualification to investigate homicides. Yet I wonder what in the world possessed them to question Smith, a leading person of interest, before interviewing any witnesses, family, and friends.

We know they interviewed him because when I tried to interview Smith again, he wouldn't talk to me. During their interview, they had told him to trust nobody except them. The only witness who said they showed up at her door told me it was after the timeframe they said they interviewed Smith.

With proper knowledge of Smith's life and personality, the quality and contents of an interview and/or an interrogation would have been more fruitful, and likely would have instilled fear, possibly evoked movement, or produced a mistake by the person of interest. A cold case analyst or investigator achieves this by examining suspect-ology and conducting a crime scene analysis.

Richard Walter and Dr. Robert Keppel originally developed four categories of homicidal offenders built on research conducted by the FBI.[29] The typologies apply to all genders, and have since been revised to encompass sexual and nonsexual murders, bringing the total of typologies to eight.

Following is my interpretation of the original four. The first category, Power Assertive, is a personality type naturally attracted to occupations like law enforcement, given the power and control that comes with the job. When I give these descriptions to law enforcement groups, they'll call out their buddies and be like, "Dude, that's so you!"

CATEGORY 1: POWER ASSERTIVE

This is the macho man, the guy at the gym who grunts while deadlifting, and then drops the weights and flexes his muscles in the mirror. This individual often drives American made cars. He is extremely homophobic, believes he is God's gift to women, and is a braggart. He will take credit for his actions. He will use opportunity and surprise to subdue a victim. If the victim is abducted from an outdoor location, their body will be moved to a secondary location. While an assault is planned, murder is not. Murder will result when the perpetrator feels that he or she is losing control over the victim. There may be beatings about the victim's face.

CATEGORY 2: POWER REASSURANCE

This is the dude who often lives in his mother's basement playing videogames at age forty-five. He's also the guy who approaches women in a park with his hand in his pocket in the shape of a gun to induce fear but doesn't have the courage to use a weapon. If a weapon is used, it will most likely come from the victim and/or his or her surroundings. A loner, he's socially awkward and a fantasizer. His past crimes may include being a peeping tom. When crimes escalate, the perpetrator imagines him or herself to be in a relationship with the victim. In sexual crimes, this perpetrator is referred to as "the gentleman rapist." If the victim is murdered, insertions may be present in the body. He will be obsessed with the crime, possibly collecting newspaper clippings about the event. He or she is also likely to take a souvenir from the victim, and quite often said souvenir will always remain in close physical proximity to the offender at all times, such as his or her pocket or vehicle. Like the power assertive offender, while an assault is planned, the murder is not and results from the offender losing control.

CATEGORY 3: ANGER RETALIATORY

This individual often has mommy issues. Not even necessarily a mother, but an overbearing, sadistic matriarchal figure who ran his life from the get-go. He hates women. Female offenders of this type are extremely rare. This is the first offender typology where both the assault and murder are planned. An excessive amount of violence will be inflicted upon victims. The signature of an Anger Retaliatory killer? He will pose his victim so her back is facing him. In his mind, this solidifies his power and control over the victim, even in death.

CATEGORY 4: ANGER EXCITATION

This last offender typology of the original four is thankfully the rarest. These are the Ted Bundys of the world. This offender takes extreme pleasure in the torture of his victims, the infliction of pain. They are exceptionally smart and usually make excellent military material, as they are very adept at compartmentalization. They're able to seamlessly transition into a charming, suave, highly functioning member of society just as they are equally able to devolve into a primal being, laser focused on the kill. In fact, one victim who escaped the deadly clutches of Ted Bundy said the change was instant and noticeable, so much so that his eyes appeared to change color. These offenders are chameleons; elusive, and extremely difficult to catch. If investigators don't use staff trained in offender typology, they will get nowhere with this individual during interrogations. He will toy with investigators like a cat with a mouse, and leave you more confused than when you came into the room. You are his target once he is captured. This typology requires a trained expert.

We believe Molly's murderer most likely falls under the Power Assertive category, and believe that murdering Molly was not the goal, but rather, the result of the perpetrator losing control.

In December 2015, I was asked by the Child Abduction Response Team to give a training to law enforcement on victimology, suspectology, and how to heat up cold cases. The training was held in Norton, Massachusetts, and was a great group of professionals. The discussion was lively and during breaks I chitchatted with the officers.

Lieutenant Daniel Richard and Trooper Nicole Morrell of the MSP decided to drop in for the presentation. They sat with arms crossed the entire time and didn't take a single note while others scribbled away. The lieutenant and trooper sat at the front, staring with blank expressions.

Following the lecture, they smiled and asked if they could take their picture with me for their Twitter page. I agreed.

The Just One Piece campaign slide was the last in my presentation. After Richard and Morrell left, and the class was winding down, one of the police chiefs was leaning against the doorway with arms crossed, glaring at them as they left the building.

"Fucking assholes. They'll smile and take their picture with you, and then won't do a damn thing and won't let you do your job," he said.

Figure 36: Lieutenant Daniel Richard, Dr. Sarah Stein, & Trooper Nicole Morrell, December 2015.

Later in my efforts, Dr. Ann Marie Mires, the director for the Molly Bish Center for the Protection of Children & the Elderly from Anna Maria College in Paxton, Massachusetts, asked for my protocols for tip campaigns and volunteer instructions so she could study them. I gladly gave them. I had known Dr. Mires since 2005; I trusted her.

Without permission, she gave my protocols to the MSP and informed me that only law enforcement should be doing these tip campaigns—the same law enforcement agency people were too afraid to talk to.

The MSP subsequently took my material and used it on another case on a significant date: the time around the fortieth anniversary of the disappearance of Andy Puglisi from South Lawrence, who disappeared while at a neighborhood pool.

On September 1, 2016, the Massachusetts State Police held a safety day at the pool from which Andy disappeared, and asked people to come forward with information.[30]

It is my understanding that little, if any information was collected that day for exactly the reasons I mentioned from the Just One Piece campaign. I've never seen so many people afraid to talk to law enforcement as I did in Massachusetts, or as many people who believed the agency to be secretive and corrupt.

Heather Bish finished her doctorate around that time, and we took her out to celebrate. We went to Mexicali, a restaurant in Ware, as Mexican is Heather's favorite. We celebrated with margaritas.

In December, I resigned from my teaching position. I tried to bounce back. But instead of taking time to process what had happened and give myself time to heal, I chose to barrel forward as if nothing was wrong, when in reality, everything, absolutely everything, was wrong.

I interviewed for the Chair of the Criminal Justice program at Anna Maria College, where the Molly Bish Center is located. I was all but guaranteed the job both verbally and in writing by members of the search committee. Much to my puzzlement, they turned around and handed it to an alumnus of the college.

I accepted a visiting professor position in Criminal Justice at Fitchburg State University for the 2016-2017 academic year. The school's criminal justice program was interesting in concept: the policing track was a five-year program. During their fifth year of education, students would attend a police academy run by Fitchburg State University and the Municipal Police Training Committee. They would also earn a master's degree in that fifth year.

My schedule that first semester was hell. I got up at 4:30 every morning for a ninety-minute commute to the university, and taught four seminar classes back to back with no break.

The department chair was Dr. Christine Shane, a fantastic lady who certainly knows how to run an academic department with an iron fist: she put up with no bullshit. I admire her greatly.

She had a policy whereby she expected faculty to be on campus five days a week, regardless of whether they had classes scheduled. So, I suffered the commute, was teaching a legal course, consulting on Molly's case along with several others. I was also suffering from depression, going to therapy, and trying to maintain my career at the same time.

In March 2017, I was offered a permanent position at Fitchburg State University. Things started to calm down.

I had the option of a job for the following year, a permanent position I first accepted and then declined for two reasons. First, I didn't agree with the university's admission standards for allowing students into the policing program who had no business being there.

The second reason I declined was because Jack and I were getting ready—to run for our lives.

I love life . . . really I do.

-MOLLY BISH

CHAPTER TEN

Transformation

For nine chapters now, I have closely scrutinized what I perceive to be the mistakes and missteps of others in Molly's investigation. Now it's time for me to own mine.

In June 2017, I had gotten Peter Massey, a former professor of mine at the University of New Haven, to agree to conduct a search at the campground for the car possibly used in the commission of Molly's abduction and murder.

The technology we planned to use to conduct the search is called ground penetrating radar. The machine is dragged over the earth and reveals any anomalies or disturbances below the surface on a screen. The machine does not show a picture of what is below the surface, but indicates a general shape. We were looking for the long, rectangular shape of a car. Jack and I finally felt we had enough circumstantial evidence and witness statements to support a search for the buried car. I obtained permission from the current landowner and Molly's family to conduct the search.

The day before the search, I went to the woods of what remained of the Old Sawmill Campground. I planned to scout the area to determine the most promising locations.

At the time of Molly's abduction, the former campground owner was leasing land to a cellphone company in order to build a cell tower. We believed that area would have been ideal for Smith to dispose of the vehicle. I marked a few other locations. The area to be searched was massive and impossible to complete in one day.

Suddenly, a truck came barreling into the clearing where I was standing. The previous campground owner hopped out. Jack and I had interviewed him previously, so he knew who I was.

"Can I help you?" I asked, watching him stand there, visibly shaking. He appeared to be extremely nervous.

"Are you guys really searching tomorrow?" he asked.

I nodded my head. "Yup, us, and the state police may be here too, just don't know yet."

I had asked the Massachusetts State Police if they wanted to send representatives just in case something was found. He paused, seemingly considering his options. Wringing his fingers and looking at the ground, he said, "Well, I didn't bury the car."

He jumped in his truck and was gone. I stood there, hearing the truck retreat, thinking, well then, who did?

We conducted the search at the campground on June 15, 2017. Professor Massey brought a team of student volunteers. Heather couldn't be present that day, as her daughter Mikaela had a college event they were attending. In her place, Heather sent a woman whom she said was helping the family with the media in her stead, along with Molly's best friend, Natalee. I wish she hadn't been there that day; I didn't want her to see this. But she came, nonetheless.

I met the alleged media woman, whom I'll call Joy. Looking back, my radar should have been going off from the second I met her. Jack's did—he hated this woman from the start. That being said, when I arrived that morning to what I thought was going to be a relatively quiet search, I arrived to a circus of chaos. Reporters were everywhere.

I allowed them to come only partway into the woods so as not to disturb the scenes we had planned to search. Eventually, I created a border using crime scene tape tied on trees to prevent more press from coming in.

The search began. Magi showed up and began giving interviews to media personnel. I was occupied supervising the search team, though extremely disappointed no one from the Massachusetts State Police had come. Heather and I texted throughout the day with her asking if anything had been found. Not yet.

We discovered masses of discarded refuse at the campground. There were heaps of metal, wood, and an abandoned trailer that had caught fire. Several witness statements said there were items like refrigerators and microwaves buried there.

Figure 37: Flags marking the search grid, 2017.

We found several areas of interest to be further explored and excavated. When we had breaks, I was running back and forth to Joy. I asked her to relay what was going on to Heather while I managed the circus. She indicated she would.

Deep in the woods, far away from the hordes of media, our team could finally conduct our work in peace. It's not that I was ungrateful that the media was there; I was thrilled that interest in Molly's investigation was still active, but I never expected as many, and I never expected them to be so aggressive.

Suddenly, I heard helicopter rotor blades. Up above was the MSP doing flyovers of the area while we were on the ground doing the search. I have no doubt they wanted to map where we were looking.

Though we did not find the car that day, we did find compelling information that needed further exploration. There was no telling the amount or range of items that lay hidden in the earth waiting to be exposed. The truth doesn't stay buried forever.

144

I was ready to call it a day when Joy ran up to me, hurriedly saying that I needed to update the press before we left. She said it was critical, and Heather had cleared it. She ushered me into a car and drove us to a nearby parking lot where she had assembled the media.

Joy towed me into the bathroom and began fixing my hair and putting lipstick on me. "Are you sure this is okay?" I asked her.

I was trembling. She assured me it was, that she had been talking to Heather all day. I am a very introverted person, so the prospect of speaking alone to a huge group of reporters terrified me. Joy opened a bottle and handed me a nip of Fireball. "Come on, it'll calm you down. Yes, it's fine. Heather knows; go tell them what you found."

I had never met this woman and yet she claimed to be Heather's best friend. Because Heather had vouched for her, I believed her. I shouldn't have. I should have called Heather, John and Magi, and told the media to wait while I conferred with the family. But I didn't.

Joy shoved me out of the bathroom and arranged the search team behind me on a makeshift podium. Lights, camera, action.

I was honest. I said that it would be up to the Massachusetts State Police and the Worcester DA's office to decide whether to excavate the site. I said we had found compelling information at the site and planned to return in the following days. It seemed as quickly as it started, it was over, and Joy suggested dinner as no one on the search team had eaten anything that day. I told Joy I had to first call Heather. She said that was no problem but wanted to get to the restaurant first.

I was exhausted, emotionally and physically drained. I was also disappointed that we hadn't found what we were looking for.

Heather was extremely disappointed, felt that I had violated her boundaries, and her trust. She told me I should be ashamed of myself because I acted no better than the Massachusetts State Police.

I understand her feeling, and if I were in her shoes, I would have lashed out as well. Yet deep down I believe Heather knows I would never do anything intentionally to hurt her. She also retracted what she had said about Joy. I was heartbroken.

In hindsight, I should have questioned Joy more aggressively and insisted on calling Heather. I had never met this woman in all my time working on Molly's case, and yet suddenly there she was, and I was expected to trust her. I should have known better but did what I was told to do. It cost me Heather's trust.

Jack, Joy, and I went to John and Magi's house immediately. Joy took responsibility for the press conference, saying she was only trying to help. She presented herself very well as a media liaison and seemed to know very well what she was doing. John and Magi were obviously quite comfortable with her.

Jack and I tried to explain that we didn't yet know exactly what we had found at the campground, but had areas of interest to search among the masses of abandoned material. Magi accused us of acting like the MSP, and not telling them what we had. We reiterated that we didn't know exactly what we had yet, which was why further exploration was needed. Heather told me in one of her text messages that I did not have her permission to continue the search.

It was a horrible night. The last thing on earth I would ever want to do is cause Molly's family one more second of grief. I fully believed Molly's family had cleared an update to the press, and I fully believed Joy had been communicating with Heather. Neither was true, but I had believed it.

On Monday, June 19, 2017, at 8:25 a.m., I sent the following email to Trooper Murphy.

[EMAIL]

Good Morning Trooper Murphy. Please find attached an additional narrative of information I received over the weekend regarding Mr. Smith – I believe it is compelling. I could really use your help today. I am meeting with the additional witness at the campground at 1:30 with her father – if you could please be there or if someone from your office could be there, I would appreciate it. Also, there is information in the report about potential physical evidence and I didn't know if you want to send crime scene services or if you want me to recover the item and deliver it to you. Feel free to call me anytime I'm around this morning. Thank you so much.

All the Best,
Sarah

Following is the supplemental report I provided.

[CASE REPORT]

Information Received Since June 15, 2017

Search for white vehicle at Old Sawmill Campground, West Brookfield, MA

Provided by: Sarah L. Stein, PhD

Introduction:

In October of 2014 Molly Bish's family and I hosted the Just One Piece tip campaign. As a result of this campaign, four individuals came forward to identify a potential person of interest in the abduction and murder of Molly Bish: Mr. Smith. Since 2014 I have been unable to exclude Mr. Smith as being a person of interest in Molly's case and have accumulated significant amounts of circumstantial evidence.

Recent Events:

According to witnesses, the former owner of the Old Sawmill Campground in West Brookfield, MA used to allow campers to either pay him to bury discarded items or bury the items themselves. Based on witness reports, I had a reasonable belief that the vehicle tied to the abduction and murder of Molly Bish, possibly a 1986 Buick LeSabre, or parts of said vehicle, were buried at the Old Sawmill Campground.

As such, I contacted the current landowner to obtain permission to search the property with a ground penetrating radar. Once I obtained permission from both Molly's family and the current landowner, I contacted Peter Massey, M.S. of The University of New Haven who had conducted many of these searches. Mr. Massey agreed to assist in the search.

On Wednesday, June 14, 2016, I went up to the campground to survey the areas of interest we would be searching. We were focusing on an area that used to be the Smith's campsite where around the time of Molly's abduction, the former campground owner was leasing land to a cellphone company to build a cellular tower.

On Wednesday, June 14, 2017, the former campground owner drove his vehicle into the campground and exited the vehicle, visibly upset and shaking. He asked me if we were going to be searching the following day. I indicated we were and quite possibly the Massachusetts State Police. This individual excitedly said, "Well, I didn't bury the car." He then quickly returned to his vehicle and left.

On Thursday, June 15, 2017, we searched the campground. Mr. Massey detected several anomalies below the surface of the earth and indicated that a significant amount of the property was filled in and there was potential for other areas of interest. In addition, we found many items disposed of on the surface of the earth to include a discarded trailer, cans of lighter fluid, etc.

Also on June 15, 2017, Kathy Curran, a reporter, visited the home of Mr. Smith, who declined to speak with her.

Also on Thursday, June 15, 2017, I was contacted by Abby Map [fictional name]. She reported to me three years ago during the Just One Piece campaign that a man in a white vehicle had been following her and her cousins and would follow their school bus every single day around the time of Molly's abduction. When Ms. Map saw the story provided by Kathy Curran, despite the blurring of Mr. Smith's face and providing no additional identifying information, Ms. Map instantly remembered that it was Mr. Smith who had followed her and her cousins; Ms. Map had camped at Old Sawmill Campground for 20 years. Ms. Map identified the vehicle as having belonged to Mr. Smith's father (now deceased).

Of note, I omitted two paragraphs for the safety of the informant.

Also on Saturday, June 17, 2017, I was contacted by Margaret Stripe [fictional name]. She purchased a home in Warren, Massachusetts, and was contacted by the MSP after Molly Bish's remains were found, as the home used to belong to a level III sex offender and at one point was a person of interest in Molly Bish's disappearance.[31]

Figure 38: Hubcap found by homeowner.

Ms. Stripe indicated that about four years ago (2013), she recovered a hubcap and said to her husband, "It almost looks like a car was taken apart here," and indicated there were other artifacts of dismantled vehicles on the property. The hubcap she saved had the Buick emblem on it, and she used it as a lawn ornament.

This residence is 4.9 miles away from the Old Sawmill Campground. From my recollection of the Bish case, 11 people failed a polygraph examination. It is possible that the former campground owner allowed this individual to stay at the campground as he let two other registered sex offenders stay there as well. It is possible Mr. Smith knew this individual, and that the vehicle used to facilitate Molly's abduction and murder was dismantled at the home and parts of it disposed at the Old Sawmill Campground.

In my professional opinion, based on the circumstantial evidence provided previously to the Massachusetts State Police, and the additional information that has surfaced, I am confident that Mr. Smith cannot be excluded as a person of interest in the abduction and murder of Molly Bish, and has displayed classic post-crime behaviors that indicate involvement in this crime.

Respectfully Submitted,

Sarah L. Stein, PhD

I heard nothing from the Massachusetts State Police. Instead, on Monday, June 19, 2017, at 3:57 p.m., I received the following email from Heather, which was also sent to Trooper Murphy.

[EMAIL FROM HEATHER BISH]

Subject: Next Steps

Good Afternoon,

Sarah, I want to thank you for your time and efforts associated with investigating Molly's case. However, after the events of this past weekend, I am asking you to refrain from any further investigations on this case. Please do not act in my family's behalf or the Molly Bish Foundation's behalf. At this time, we are regrouping in our efforts to locate the person who did this to Molly and feel that we (sic) moving in another direction. Although, we appreciate your drive and initiative, it is no longer needed on our behalf. We are grateful for all of your time and the efforts you invested into this case.

Thank you,

Heather Bish

I couldn't catch my breath, I couldn't understand. No further contact, no further explanation, nothing, literally ripped my heart apart. I was sitting at home and began to sob; the deep, gut-wrenching sobs that can only come from the depths of your soul.

I had done everything, everything for these people, for Molly. Yes, I shouldn't have given in to Joy's pressure, but I never wanted anything except to get justice for Molly Bish.

I wrote this book because our system is broken, particularly in Massachusetts. It is broken in how victims, families and witnesses are treated. It's also broken in how consultants with expert training and doctorate degrees are treated, all because of politics.

The next day, I dragged myself out to get the mail. I had been told that Smith obtained an attorney. Our darling mail lady was delivering our mail to our door so I wouldn't have to walk down our 500-foot driveway to get it. When she passed the stack of mail into my hands, I saw the return address and began to shake. Mr. Smith. He had printed up a no-trespass order and sent it to me certified.

I signed and returned the receipt. Our mail lady knew who I was and could see how distressed I was. The next day, the mail was on the porch, along with two cans of bear spray held together by a rubber band with a note attached.

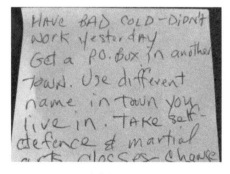

"Have bad cold—Didn't work yesterday. Get a P.O. Box in another town. Use different name in town you live in. Take self-defense & martial arts classes. Change appearance."

Figure 39: Note left by mail personnel.

That gesture meant more to me than anything. At least someone in town was concerned about me.

Going back to the abstract I delivered about celebrity deviancy, how it would follow a particularly successful period in that individual's life and that the type of shaming they experience, reintegrative, which is recognizing what the person did might not have been correct, but that the person in and of themselves was decent, versus disintegrative stigmatization, which is identifying the whole person as evil, will affect their path. My very own abstract had become my reality.

I started getting calls from producers, the press, newsrooms such as CNN, and more families asking for help. Random strangers began approaching me in town, asking about the status of Molly's case and asking what was taking so long.

I didn't know what to say. These residents had invested their own hearts, souls, time and money into Molly's case. I felt helpless, gagged. I had no answers for them because I couldn't understand it myself. I was no longer my own person. I became the face of Molly's case, an investigation I could no longer investigate.

Joy infiltrated my life again, begging me to take on the case of Holly Piirainen. She felt Molly and Holly were connected, and said she hadn't shared the information she had with anyone else and wanted to give it to me.

I cared deeply about Holly and had met members of her family throughout the years. They supported the Bish family by attending Molly's vigils and many other events held for her. I inquired about Holly, and was told they had their own consultants, and not to worry about them. When I learned the truth, that Holly's family had little to no help since she vanished on August 5, 1993, I was crushed. Why hadn't I just asked them directly whether they needed help?

Why did I believe what I was told? Because back then I had faith in the system.

When Holly's family and I met officially, I cried and apologized profusely. They welcomed me with open arms, were compassionate, kind, and understanding that there was only so much I could do.

We held two tip campaigns, one in October 2017, and one, which included the first vigil ever held for Holly in October 2018, just before Jack and I moved away from Massachusetts.

The other connection between Holly and Molly was Joy, who claimed she was Holly's camp counselor just before she vanished. Joy explained that at the end of each camp session, the children put on a skit. She said that it was ten-year-old Holly's idea to do a skit about what to do if you get kidnapped, and that Holly allegedly said, "If I ever get taken, I'm going to leave a shoe."

When Holly disappeared shortly after, all that remained of her was a shoe. An interesting fact is that Joy's grandparents had a house nearby, and Joy was on the road where Holly was abducted the very day she went missing. Joy and Heather then become best friends, and then Molly went missing.

Joy claimed a drug connection and a campground connection linked the two cases. She further alleged that the Massachusetts State Police knew about it.

My head, my heart felt like it was about to explode. I couldn't handle it anymore. Was the information that was being given to me real, a ploy by Heather and/or Joy to get rid of me, drive me crazy, or both? Was it a complete coincidence? I'll never know. What I do know is that I was spiraling fast.

In November 2017, our faith was renewed that the truth about the MSP brass and Worcester DA's office was about to be exposed. A story appeared on November 16, 2017, headlined, "Just Like We Said, Government Officials Claim DA Joe Early Communicated Directly with Colonel McKeon to Redact Alli Bibaud's Arrest Report."[32]

Colonel Richard McKeon fell on his sword for Early and retired. I have no doubt he authorized changes to the arrest report of the judge's daughter for driving under the influence because he was fearful his political appointment would be taken away if he said no to Joe Early, Worcester's district attorney.

Early was up for re-election in 2018. The DA's opponent in 2018, was a man named Blake Rubin. Early was re-elected by a two-to-one margin. Rubin has since been indicted for witness intimidation and conspiracy charges.[33]

After Colonel McKeon retired, the MSP needed damage control. They needed the antithesis of McKeon, someone who would promote their dedication to resolving cold cases.

That person was Colonel Kerry Gilpin, who replaced Colonel McKeon on November 15, 2017.[34] Colonel Gilpin brought a unique perspective to her newly found position: Her own sister, fifteen-year-old Tracy Gilpin, had been murdered in October 1986. The MSP was in charge of the investigation. Tracy's alleged killer was arrested in March 2018.[35] Below is an excerpt from the article noted on the prior page that was published on November 16, 2017.

[ARTICLE EXCERPT]

"During the interviews, Hand, formerly a Kingston resident, made statements to investigators that could be construed as admissions to the crime, authorities said.

Our suspect Smith had made similar statements to me, Jack, and several witnesses. Yet despite that plus the mountain of circumstantial evidence against him, he wasn't charged.

In July 2018, Colonel Gilpin was kind enough to grant me and Holly's family a meeting with her and MSP staff from the Hampden detective unit at MSP headquarters in Framingham.

That meeting was significantly different than those I had experienced previously with the Massachusetts State Police. Colonel Gilpin was compassionate; kind and respectful towards Holly's family, and she was quite kind to me. It was clear from that meeting that she took these investigations extremely seriously, and made it a point to meet with several families of murder victims during her tenure. She even established a new Unresolved Case Unit with the agency prior to her retirement.

Holly's family and I held a vigil in October 2018. Colonel Gilpin came, as did Captain Christopher Wilcox, and Trooper Thomas Sullivan. Joy also came, claiming she hadn't been able to talk to me over the past year because Heather would have disowned her as a friend. She also said she was actually doing me a huge favor. Jack was livid that she had shown up. I told Trooper Sullivan that he might want to have a chat with her.

One particularly interesting thing that came out of the tip campaign was a letter delivered to me at the Sturbridge Host Hotel that demonstrates the undeniable fear residents have of the MSP.

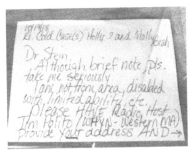 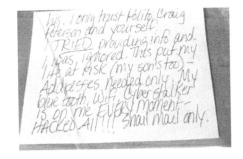

Figure 40: Anonymous letter.

In December 2017, Jack had planned a golfing trip to Florida with his buddies. I hate December. My mother died December 13. It's not a happy month for me.

When Jack and I first began seeing each other, he did his very best to give the joy of Christmas back to me, the kind of Christmas joy he had growing up as a child, with a tree, stories of magic and reindeer, and a happy family. For Christmas 2014, Jack took me to Yankee Candle and bought us our first ornament.

After my mother died, my family and I almost always traveled for the holidays, often to warm, tropical, faraway places that didn't remind us all of cold, darkness, and death. When Jack planned his trip to Florida in 2017, I thought I'd be fine at home. I planned to read, play with the dogs, and watch TV.

The night before Jack left, I remembered already feeling alone, and desperately sad. Jack's a morning person and likes to schedule that first flight out so he can enjoy a fuller day at his destination. Me, not so much. Mornings are my nemesis. So, when Jack got up to leave at around 4:30 a.m., I saw him out the door. Then I was alone. Alone on eight acres of woods surrounding me, the bitter darkness of winter swallowing me up.

Our house in Ware was designed in an odd way with the master suite added to the original frame. As such, our bedroom was on the ground floor, while the living room and kitchen were upstairs.

I hated that master suite after two personal traumas: resigning from my teaching position, and being dismissed from Molly's case. I felt extremely exposed and vulnerable. Our driveway was such that it basically came right up to the house and there was nowhere to go except out our backdoor in the master suite and into the woods. I felt safe upstairs on our couch. It was a huge, plush wraparound that sat in the corner of the living room where there were no windows. I could have a vantage point of anyone coming at me.

I stood at our kitchen sink looking out at the wintry tundra as Jack's taillights flickered and faded, bound for sunny Florida. I went to the freezer, got out a shot glass, and poured Absolut Citron until it touched the glass brim. It was warm and tingly sliding down my throat and warming my belly. Suddenly, the world felt hazy, soft, and less frightening. I curled up on the couch with my weighted blanket and went to sleep.

That week was the thirtieth anniversary of my mother's death. It was also the anniversary of when I left my university job where I worked with Jack. I couldn't begin to face all the failures. Though they weren't entirely my own, I felt they were. I was in so much pain. All I wanted to do was sleep the week away. I didn't want to feel a thing.

Although I was only four at the time, I couldn't save my mother. I dreamed about her death the night it happened. I dreamed I was standing in my grandparents' driveway, and my mother's car was parked. I dreamed an ambulance came to the driveway. Then it attached to my mother's car like a tow truck. The ambulance backed up and turned right towards the hospital. I was spending the night at my grandparents the night my mother died. I was sleeping on their couch. I woke up, seeing the embers in the fireplace just starting to go out. It was still pitch black out. It was snowing and thundering. I remember pressing my fingers against the window in the living room. I knew she was gone.

I felt like a failure after I left my academic position.

I felt like I had failed Molly.

I felt like I had failed myself. I was confused, sad, angry, and in agonizing pain, sobbing every time I woke up.

Why I didn't just reach out to my family, who loves me more than anything in the world? I don't know. Probably because I have felt my entire life that I needed to protect them, that I needed to be perfect. It was unacceptable to me to be anything except collected, poised, in control, sensible, and professional.

I was none of those things that week, and I regret it bitterly. I even ripped the dragonfly off our wall. What I don't regret is that the experience I was about to endure would forever transform me, forever strengthen me, and save my life. I wasn't really living, and would have died if I had let those demons take me down.

Jack returned home on Saturday. On Sunday, we went to church as always. I felt horrible and looked worse. During communion, my hand began to shake slightly. I told Jack I wasn't feeling well, and we headed home. The last thing I remember was the sun bothering me, flickering through the bare winter trees.

The next thing I remember was waking up in the hospital. I had suffered a grand mal seizure. Hating hospitals, I demanded to go home. I should have stayed and spared Jack the agony of the next few days. That night, as we laid down to go to bed, I remember Jack coming into the bedroom, I remember smiling at him, and then nothing.

I woke up to medics standing over me. They asked me who the president was. They asked me what day it was. They asked me if I wanted to go to the hospital. No! They left. Jack started to come back to bed, and I felt my arms begin to go rigid again. "Call them back, call them back!" I screamed. "Am I dying?" I sobbed.

"No, no you're not dying!" Jack called to me as he sprinted for his phone.

Then, blackness.

I spent three days in the hospital. I had to learn how to walk again. I bit my tongue so hard during a seizure that it was black and bruised for almost three months. The doctors determined that my magnesium level was so low, seizures were inevitable. When all I wanted to do was escape, this was a hell of a reality to come back to.

I remember the day I broke down and finally faced my pain—all of it: from my mother, to my resignation from my teaching position, and finally, Molly.

What broke me that week was my inability to believe, and further, accept the reality I found myself living in. It was unfathomable to me that the institution of justice, on a fundamental level, was broken. The core of my being has always been, and always will be the values of justice: equality for all, honor, integrity, and at a bare minimum, always trying to do the right thing, with good intention.

The image of these ideals I held, the principles by which I had tried to live my life, seemed to dissolve beneath my feet, leaving me with no ground to stand on. I literally could not comprehend what had happened to Molly, nor what had happened to me. I could not reconcile the fact that the system I had believed in so fervently, our justice system, had evaporated right before my eyes—if it had ever existed at all.

I didn't make a historical cross-country road trip as Molly and John planned to do, but I've been driving on a highway of experience going one hundred miles per hour for nearly two decades, and the journey has been incredible. I think I had it right all along, in my journal entry in 2004 regarding the anti-crime rally John and I attended.

[JOURNAL ENTRY]

2004

The profoundness of the event came upon realizing that this is how change happens, not legislation or signing the AMBER Alert Bill, but this: communities banding together to bring their children safety and a brighter future in what has become such a bleak and dark world.

When I said that the air at that event was alive, it was. It was electric, bright, beautiful, and peaceful energy. A collective call for justice. For *everyone*.

As Jack wrote in his email to Joe Quinlan, "Other than Whitey Bulger and the Boston bombing, this (Molly) case has consumed more Commonwealth resources than any other."

Molly was blonde-haired and blue-eyed and from a well-to-do, politically connected family. That wasn't her fault. The news coverage her case received compared to other victims? Also, not her fault. Her legacy lives on to this day, and I believe it is with good reason. Molly did ultimately serve as a lifeguard, first by protecting thousands of children through the Molly Bish Foundation. She went on to save *my* life by shattering illusions and ideals, replacing them with brutal truths. Beyond that, she is going to continue to save countless other lives because of what she can teach us:

Don't make assumptions. This of course goes for everyone, but particularly for law enforcement. Don't assume that just because a kid has smoked a joint or two, they just wandered away from a brand-new job to toke up in the woods. Don't assume that she drowned. Listen! She was the best swimmer in her class. She wouldn't go in the water without her shoes. Don't assume stereotypes that are associated with ages, races, and genders.

We are all Americans, and we *all* deserve justice. The tenth amendment of the United States Bill of Rights declares:

"The powers not delegated to the United States by the Constitution, nor prohibited by it to the states, are reserved to the states respectively, or to the people."[36]

Or to the people.

We are the people.

Remember what district attorney John Conte said about Molly? "We're just one piece of information away from solving this case."

We, America, are that *just one piece.* Remember that I said I had to carve out my own career? We must carve out our own justice because no one is going to do it for us. We must be loud, be brave, and be the voice for those who no longer have one. We must. If we do not, cases like Molly's will proliferate. Cases like Zion Butler, a five-year-old African American boy who drowned in Sacramento, California over Memorial Day 2020 will grow in number. His Mother wailed on television, "When we told them our child was missing, they told us to wait! That they were busy!"[37]

We are the people. And the people are not being heard.

Though the dialogue is beginning, we are a hell of a long way from *justice for all.*

Molly taught me that justice is not equal for all. She showed me that it wasn't even equal for her! A young blonde-haired, blue-eyed Caucasian female from suburbia. Remember the article I referenced regarding the arrest of Tracy Gilpin's alleged killer? That there was no DNA evidence yet the alleged killer was charged given the mountain of circumstantial evidence against him? As far as I'm concerned, Smith should have been in cuffs and charged in Molly's case. Yet that didn't happen. I still don't know why.

Molly taught me that life is short and can shatter in an instant. In learning that lesson, I conquered my fear of telling this story. I was afraid for years. Afraid of what would happen if I told the truth. Now, I'm more afraid of what will happen if I don't. We *all* have a responsibility, and an opportunity at our very fingertips: An opportunity for meaningful change.

No one likes change. It can be uncomfortable, stressful, and often painful. But Molly taught me something else: out of the most profound pain can emerge the most awe-inspiring change—her symbol, the dragonfly means transformation.

Jack's foreword spoke about the analogy of a crime scene being like a puzzle. I'd like to take that a step further. Our criminal justice system, our response to unresolved cases, is a hot mess of puzzle pieces right now. There is no picture to work from, no edges to follow, and no colors to separate.

While this is daunting, it's also an opportunity. Dr. Thomas Arzt, my father's dear friend who recently died said, "We have to learn how to deal with existential insecurity, uncertainty, and ambivalence, because at the center of anxiety something may want to speak to us— the way of what is to come."

I sit here wondering about the hundreds of thousands of victims who *weren't* Molly. Cory, Judy, Garrett, Theresa, Holly, Darrell, China, the list goes on. Molly's case is one of the highest profile investigations in the country and it *still* hasn't been solved. What the hell is happening to the rest of them? We can't silently sit by and let these cases languish. We can't.

Carl Jung said, "Find out what a person fears most, and that is where he will develop next."

We as a collective have feared facing changes in our justice system for decades.

The only reason J. Edgar Hoover, the infamous director of the FBI, stayed in power was because he blackmailed everyone. We've had corruption in our criminal justice system *that long*. While officers who are corrupt are few and far between, the system for which they work is antiquated and ineffective.

We don't need more bureaucracies, we need experts to work together with law enforcement. We need people who aren't going to back down because of political pressure. Further, we need term limits. Term limits for district attorneys, for chiefs of police or sheriffs, directors of federal agencies, and, most importantly, for those whom we elect to serve us in the United States congress and senate.

The late Robin Williams suggested one way to hold congress accountable was to force them to dress like NASCAR drivers and have the names of their sponsors written all over them. I love that. It is ironic that the inherent problem in the criminal justice system is the very thing that most criminals seek: power. Power corrupts. How many times do we have to learn this lesson?

We became passive regarding justice when we started allowing politicians to win elections by instilling us with fear, and accepting their word that they had all the solutions. Their only solution was to make us all afraid of society. We cannot allow this divisiveness to continue plaguing us. All the officers who are taking a knee around the country represent 99% of law enforcement. It's the system of power that must be dismantled and rebuilt by the people, and *for* the people. Is this an insurmountable feat? I think not.

I still believe in the good of people.

I believe we *will* collectively make this transformation because I cannot believe otherwise. We do not have a choice in the matter. As much as I did not have a choice in my fate according to the man on the Great Wall of China, we as a country do have a choice, and we need to make it right now. Are we going to continue to accept the status quo, or are we going to transform?

Let's transform into something better.

We must recognize law enforcement as professionals. As such, we must educate and pay them accordingly. The average salary for a police officer as of May 2020, is $56,000.[38] This is the same salary I made as a full-time professor, which is also abysmal. I believe an undergraduate degree at least should be required to become a police officer in the U.S. and require continuous training and evaluation for duty throughout a career.

As a society we must decide what we want from our law enforcement. We can't expect police to handle *everything*, although they often do because other agencies fail to do their jobs adequately.

The high-profile case of young Bella Bond in Massachusetts, reflected this fact. The little girl's body washed ashore on Deer Island in Boston on June 25, 2015. Bella was initially named Baby Doe. When her real identity was discovered, it was also revealed that the Department of Children and Families in Massachusetts, had two reports on Bella regarding child abuse, but the cases had been closed.[39]

The mother's boyfriend was eventually found responsible for Bella's death, and Bella's mother received credit for time served and probation in exchange for her testimony against her boyfriend.

I volunteered with the Department of Children and Families in Massachusetts. I submitted reports that indicated drug use in homes, and the children whose cases I was assigned were *never* removed from the custody of their parents. It was unbelievable and disheartening, and I know many police officers feel this same way.

We must identify what law enforcement represents to the American people. Are they soldiers, social workers, priests? What do we want? While I was never a law enforcement officer, I can speak to how overwhelming it is to fulfill all those roles.

When I consulted for families, I was expected to be a warrior for justice, a therapist, a friend, and more. It was exhausting and I burned out. Just like a lot of police officers do.

So, this task falls to us, the people.

When I was a teenager, I used to think my mother was so cynical. She'd always tell me, "You can never count on anyone in life except yourself."

We need to count on ourselves now, to rise above and find ways to continue this dialogue with as little loss of life as possible. Too much life has been lost already.

I am reminded of the only dream I ever had about Molly. It was summer, and she was sitting on the hill behind Comins Pond. I was standing on the beach and walked up the hill. She was sitting with her knees pulled into her chest, wearing blue jeans, a white sweater, and an old fashioned yellow rain slicker. "How are you?" I asked, sitting down beside her.

It began to rain. She shook her head softly, "Not good."

Molly got up, extending her hand to me. I took it. We walked together in silence down the same path she took with her killer. When we got to the end of the path, I woke up. We're not doing good right now, but we can do better, and Molly helped us learn how.

Hope is the thing with feathers
That perches in the soul,
And sings the tune without the words,
And never stops at all,

And sweetest in the gale is heard;
And sore must be the storm
That could abash the little bird
That kept so many warm.

I've heard it in the chillest land,
And on the strangest sea;
Yet, never, in extremity,
It asked a crumb of me.

EMILY DICKINSON

Looking back

When I was little, there was a tiny Chinese restaurant where I used to go with my parents. It was a wonderful, warm respite from the bitterly cold winters. I remember eating many wonderful dinners there with my family. We would have dumplings to start, and my mom always ordered crispy duck with plum sauce.

At the end of the meal, there was always fortune cookies. I love reading the fortunes but loathe the cookies—they're too sharp. One evening, over green tea and fortune cookies, my father raised his eyeglasses and squinted to read his fortune. It read, "Look afar, and see the end in the beginning."

If I had taken the time to do that, to stop, breathe, and really think about it, is this what I would have chosen to do with my life? According to the man who read my face on the Great Wall of China, I didn't really have a choice in the matter. This was my destiny.

I suppose this is the end of our path together, Molly and me, or perhaps it is only the beginning. I wish I had taken that advice on the fortune cookie—to look afar and see the end in the beginning. If I had, what could have gone differently on Molly's case?

Many consultants worked on Molly's case, and many have silently gone away. There's a reason for that. I should have never thought that I could be the one who would be different, get justice for Molly, and fix a broken system.

By that same token, I've always taken on exceptional challenges, and charge right in. I suppose that's why Papa said I could never work for a bureaucracy. I refuse to settle for mediocrity. I had to take a much needed breather because this job is exhausting, painful, and sometimes traumatizing.

What is horrific is that victims' families can't take a break. Molly's family can't slow down. Holly's family can't take a breather because if they do, the quest for justice will languish. They must endure their pain and still present well enough to the media to get coverage. They walk a razor-thin wire with district attorneys and correlating detectives. Many Massachusetts families I worked with told me they were afraid of angering those who worked on their loved one's case, for fear that it wouldn't get solved.

We do need some politics to succeed. We need legislation to address the nation's cold case crisis. We have over 40,000 unidentified dead in morgues and upwards of 250,000 unsolved homicides in this country.[40] We also need scientists who can help advance the various disciplines of forensics. In Molly's investigation, around 2012, district attorney Joe Early began announcing that he was sending out items from Molly's case to be tested for DNA evidence. First it was twenty-one items,[41] then it was twenty-four items in 2016.[42]

In 2017, Kathy Curran from WCVB reported the following quote from the DA regarding whether anything had materialized from the testing. "Yes, I can't speak to it in detail, but I have cause for optimism based on some of the things we've tested."[43]

In 2019, Heather Bish was quoted in the Cape Cod Times as follows: "Molly has an unidentified DNA sample in her evidence."[44]

Heather is currently pursuing getting legislation passed in the commonwealth of Massachusetts that would allow for familial DNA searching. It's hopeful that the sample in Molly's case could be explored using this technique.[45] Yet none of the coverage about the 20th anniversary mentions anything about having a DNA profile. District attorney Early has done this over and over—he says he's sending things for testing then no one hears a damn thing. There's no accountability.

There have been remarkable successes in solving cold cases using genealogy databases, and I do hope this could be an option for Molly.

After leaving Massachusetts, I decided that maybe a new career altogether would be better, so I got my real estate license. There was a bright, bubbly twenty-something in my real estate class. I looked at her with so much compassion for the wake-up call life would inevitably give her; the moment when she stops drinking the Kool-Aid, opens her eyes, and starts to question the world around her. That used to be me, I thought. I sold real estate for three months.

Today, I consult exclusively for law enforcement pro bono. I do this for a myriad of reasons, but the primary one is that law enforcement does not have the funding, the manpower, or often times the training necessary to address their cases. Many of my colleagues will not look at a case unless they receive a retainer which can range anywhere from $5,000 to $10,000. Most families, most law enforcement agencies do not have such resources. The experts who are in this field and available to help must be willing to do so at a reduced cost or no cost until law enforcement can be properly funded.

The second reason for consulting exclusively for law enforcement is the need to have access to the entirety of the case files. Not having access is a death sentence, particularly in cold cases. To conduct a thorough review, one must have access to all relevant materials.

The third reason I now work only with law enforcement is because the approach many consultants take, including the one I took in Molly's case, automatically creates a contentious relationship between the consultant and the investigating agency. In law enforcement's eyes, this approach can be perceived as a lack of confidence on the family's part, and overconfidence on the consultant's part.

I understand why the Massachusetts State Police felt the way they did about me early on. In their eyes, I was a pain in their ass, a liability. As a lowly graduate student, of course they would scoff and want to make me go away as fast as possible. However, once I obtained my doctorate and established myself as a professional in the fields of criminal justice and forensics, I was treated exactly the same way I had been when I was twenty-two. My education, training, and experience were all irrelevant to them. If anything, the MSP appeared to grow more resentful of my involvement.

That being said, I support forward thinking law enforcement wholeheartedly. Jack and I consult with the sheriff's department where we now live, and it has been an enormously fruitful working relationship. I want to support the investigators who are looking into these cases, to offer whatever expertise I can, and help them find closure. I prefer being in the background; sitting in a conference rooms sorting through boxes stuffed with files is just fine.

A friend recently asked how our new place was. Sunshine and palm trees, I answered her that it wasn't too bad. She retorted, "What, you didn't want to stay in Massachusetts and bang your head against a fucking brick wall with the state police every day?"

I leaned my head back against the headrest and smiled, shaking my head. "No. No, I really didn't."

There was a moment of silence between us. She knew all I had done. She was one of the few I trusted in the end, and she understood that I couldn't fight that battle anymore.

Before Jack and I left Massachusetts, I went to see John Bish one final time. I couldn't leave without saying goodbye to the man who had trusted me with his Molly, his heart. John's stroke left him with significant short-term memory loss. So, while a conversation five minutes ago may elude him, John tragically remembers the moment Molly went missing. The agonizing years, bringing her home, sitting in the church overnight with her casket—he remembers all of it with crystal clarity.

He also remembers the day we met. I didn't think it made that much of an impression on him. Yet, every time he saw Jack, he would tell him the same story of how John and I met, where we met, and what we did that day.

I walked up the steps to John and Magi's front porch to say good-bye. At first it seemed as though no one was home when I knocked. After again knocking softly, John appeared at the door.

"Come in, sweetheart, come in. Magi's at a doctor's appointment, but I'm sure she'd love to see you," he welcomed me in.

The house was silent and somehow seemed much colder, emptier than I remembered. John sat down in his chair, looking out the front window, as if in a dream. "This is my life now," he sighed heavily. "I watch the birds, I pick up bottles for recycling, feed the squirrels."

I didn't know how to answer him. "John, I'm so sorry. Jack and I are leaving."

"Oh, like a vacation?" he asked.

"No, John, we're leaving," I said softly. "We won't be coming back to Massachusetts."

"Oh," he whispered, looking down at his hands. "Oh, I think that's good honey, that's good…I know….I know…" he patted my hand as tears started slipping down my cheeks.

"John, I'm sorry," I whispered.

"You did everything you could," he replied.

I stood up and walked towards the door. I turned to say goodbye and found John behind me. He grabbed me and hugged me harder than he ever had. "I love you," he murmured.

"I love you, John. And I love Molly. I will never forget."

We stood in a silent embrace before I pulled away. Walking away from that house and seeing the sign that remained in their yard was excruciating.

But Molly was no longer missing; she had come home. Not in the way anyone had hoped, but Molly did come home—she came home because of a retired police officer and a local hunter.

I'd done all I could, battling an intrinsically secretive bureaucracy, being mocked by elite members of an agency who threatened to charge me with obstruction of justice countless times, denigrate and insult Jack, one of their own, and unconsciously obstructing justice themselves, again, because of politics. We can do better than this. We can and *must* do better.

After Ashley and Miranda were found, I got the idea in college to start a nonprofit organization called A.S.H.M.I.R., an acronym that combined the girls' names and stood for America Should Handle Missing (Persons) Investigations Responsibly. I remember holding a fundraiser in my dorm. I had high hopes back then. I still do, though not naïve hopes any longer.

Figure 41: Sign outside the Bish home.

I hope Molly will get justice. I hope Holly will get justice. I hope every victim gets justice. For Molly, I am unsure what the end result will be, but her case most likely will remain officially unsolved for a couple reasons. First, the crime scene, the site of her abduction, was inadvertently destroyed by well-meaning searchers whom law enforcement allowed onto the beach, thinking that Molly had simply wandered off or drowned, as admitted by district attorney Joe Early.[46] There have also been so many publicly identified persons of interest in Molly's case, to include Smith, that any decent defense attorney would be able to discredit the merits of a particular suspect at trial, short of physical evidence linking the suspect directly to the crime. Though that, too, could be argued away. Molly's remains, and bathing suit laid exposed in the elements for almost three years. Anyone's DNA could have been deposited; it doesn't necessarily mean he committed the crime, does it?

The ouroboros tattoo I got at seventeen on the day Molly Bish was abducted, symbolized myself, my soul, and represents the amazing capacity of the human spirit to be resilient and evolve through the seasons of life, such as they are.

The dragonfly tattoo I got on Molly's twenty-first birthday, after I had met her family, symbolized that I would always keep a space in myself for her; that I'd never forget.

I regret neither image. I do not know why the paths of the dragonfly and the ouroboros became enmeshed; maybe it was fate, cosmic destiny. Maybe it was coincidence. I choose to believe the stars aligned, and there was a reason I was meant to make that trek from Washington, D.C. to Warren, Massachusetts, when I was twenty-one years old, even if that reason has yet to be revealed.

What I do know is that Molly knows that countless people love her and tried to give her justice—too many to name here. What I also choose to believe is that Molly came to Jack, and then to me, to tell us that we found the man responsible for her abduction and murder.

Why do I believe such a thing? Two days after we interviewed Smith, Jack decided to take a motorcycle ride to Comins Pond. He wanted to take a panoramic photograph to frame and give to me as a gift. When he got to our house and got off his bike, his face was white. "What's the matter?" I asked him.

He showed me the photograph.

Figure 42: Photo by Retired MSP Detective Lieutenant John W. Drawec, Esq. Oct. 2014)

In the right corner one can see the light burst. Look hard enough and one can see what looks like legs— possibly two pairs—in the lower right corner. Jack told me there was no reason the photo would come out like that, as the day was perfectly clear. I think it was Molly, and who knows, maybe Holly, coming to tell us that we had done it—we had found the man responsible.

That is what I choose to believe, and I also choose to believe that even though Molly may not get justice in this lifetime, karma certainly gave her some measure of peace: Smith died on June 26, 2019, nineteen years to the day that Magi and Molly saw the man in the white car in the parking lot at Comins Pond.

So, there it is, the story of my investigation into the abduction and murder of sixteen-year-old Molly Bish. My maternal grandfather in Texas, told me, "Darlin', a colleague of mine once told me, be sure you know what you're aiming at before you swing, otherwise you could miss it by a square mile."

I fully concede that I may be missing this by a square mile. This text is a fraction of the information stored in my files, and probably less than what is housed within the secretive walls of the Worcester DA's office and Massachusetts State Police. If I had ever had access to their information, my assessment, and ultimate conclusion may have been very different.

Who knows what the next chapter will bring, but I am guided by the words of Mahatma Gandhi: "Truth never damages a cause that is just."[47]

BY JOHN W. DRAWEC, ESQ.

AFTERWORD

Because of this book, I would expect that the reader has had an awakening into a less than perfect justice system. Those words are not an attack on any person, office, or organization. If the system was perfect, then a suspect would have been identified, arrested, tried, and convicted in Molly's case years ago.

The sad thing is Molly's case is not alone. There are hundreds of thousands of unresolved cases in the United States. I was once interviewed by the media as a forensic science expert soon after a suspect was identified and arrested on a local decades-old unresolved homicide case after he was identified through advanced DNA testing. In the interview, I made a comment that because of advanced technologies, it is probably easier to solve many unresolved cases now decades later. That said, scientific advancements in the forensic sciences are only some of the tools that are available to contemporary investigators.

Advanced DNA testing was not available when many of these crimes were committed. Modern advancements may require the need to reexamine evidence in many of these cases. This should be done by a trained forensic scientist. Advancements in the discovery of evidence is progressing with such instruments as the M-Vac® device.

In some jurisdictions, legislation opened genealogy databases and allows for investigators to narrow in on suspects through their familial DNA. There have even been advancements in getting DNA from old fingerprint lifts that were previously unusable, through "touch" DNA.

These advancements may assist investigators in getting that one piece they need for an indictment and, more importantly, justice.

Technology alone is not the answer, though. The need for a complete and thorough investigation is paramount for success. One of my MSP mentors was Major Dan Jamroz, who ran tactical operations. Together, we taught incident response throughout New England to state police agencies. Dan often used the phrase, "Know what's in your toolbox," or know what resources are available to you.

In major incidents under Major Jamroz' command, the MSP used a *force package* approach allowing the release of all Tac Ops resources (Air Wing, K-9, Mounted, Special Emergency Response team, Tactical EMTs, etc.) for major incidents. The idea was to throw every resource available at the beginning to hopefully achieve a quick and successful outcome. It proved effective, yet this approach was not used at crime scenes because they didn't fall under Tac Ops. If the approach is effective, why not use it at crime scenes?

Sarah's Child Abduction Response Team used parallel investigations as an approach. If a child went missing and it was unclear whether there had been an abduction, they would conduct parallel investigations. You can investigate whether a child has runaway while simultaneously investigating the possibility of an abduction. Had that been done in Molly's case, the crime scene may well have been preserved rather than accessed by dozens of first responders and civilians who had no idea how to preserve a major crime scene.

The approach includes investigators and educated experts who study human behavior and can immediately conduct a victimology assessment. If the investigation subsequently shows that the child was not abducted and was located, no harm done. Yet, if there has been an abduction, the investigation has started off correctly.

When I served as the Education Committee Chair for the Northeastern Association of Forensic Sciences, I coordinated an educational session at a regional meeting in Atlantic City. One speaker was the commander of a homicide unit in New Jersey. He related that when someone is transferred into the unit, they were required to read every unresolved case file. Their unresolved caseload was significantly lower than the U.S. average. A fresh set of objective eyes on a case could be the answer.

That association had some of the brightest minds in the forensic sciences. Unlike me, most were not trained law enforcement investigators, rather, they were civilian scientists and practitioners with various backgrounds and education who knew their disciplines.

Many are pioneers in forensic science. Many have found the one piece that resulted in a conviction through innovative thinking within their discipline. I learned to respect them for their knowledge, their expertise, and their friendship.

When I was in Agawam, we worked in partnership with the forensic scientists who worked in our lab. We did many trainings for local officers in advancements of techniques and methodologies. I wasn't afraid that anyone would take over our job. We had plenty of work. It was a no-brainer. I wanted them to bring us quality evidence, not something that was useless. It would make it not only easier for us, but more likely to get justice in their case.

Sarah and I now do consulting for law enforcement agencies. There are such differences in philosophies from one agency to another. One agency gave us our own conference room with keycard access throughout the building. They wheeled in all the binders of case reports. They needed help and they opened all the stops for us.

In each case, we read every word. It takes us weeks, if not months. Once, when we completed one particular case, the ranking officer had tears in his eyes. It was his bottom-drawer case. Sarah had identified the *why*. They knew one particular guy was a suspect, but why him alone and not one of the other suspects? It was through Sarah's expertise in victimology that led them to the answer.

The other suspects were not as invested in the victim, nor did they exhibit the post-crime behavior that this one continued to do. The case was over forty years old.

It goes without saying that agencies shouldn't open their doors to anyone who offers to help, as they risk getting a suspect trying to interject themselves, which is post-crime behavior. There are qualified individuals who stand at the ready to assist in investigations. Know what is in your toolbox. Know where you need help and then, please, ask for it.

I have seen the frustration of many of these victims' families personally. Their anguish is awful. They long for updates, or at least a call to let them know that the case is still being actively investigated. Yet, many have gotten nothing as years pass by. These families only want answers as to who took their loved one from them.

There are too many unsolved homicides and, as a result, there are too many families with unanswered questions. The need for legislation to better fund investigators, increase training, bring in qualified experts, and advance technology appeared long ago. Investigators are not the godsend that many think they are. Three years in uniform does not make you a homicide detective, nor does twenty years for that matter. I have worked with many officers at the street level who are phenomenal investigators, and seen many seasoned officers with little investigative abilities.

There is a need for training, education, and most importantly the requirement of working together cordially and respectfully with a team of experts from various backgrounds and disciplines.

Investigators are human. They work these cases with vigor, but they are not experts in every aspect of forensic sciences, informational evidence, and/or behavioral analysis. Police focus on suspectology. They focus on getting the bad guy. That is a good thing. We need that; however, the same officers cannot be expected to know every aspect and technique of each forensic discipline. Scientists and trained, educated professionals know their abilities and limitations. It is when law enforcement realizes those limitations, the need to fill in those gaps with the appropriate experts arises.

There needs to be a mechanism in place for families to be able to seek outside help if a case remains unresolved. After all, what are the investigators missing? What new forensic techniques might be able to find that one new piece that is needed? There needs to be new eyes periodically looking at these cases. There needs to be forensic science experts going through case files to determine whether modern, more advanced testing can be used to obtain new evidence. There needs to be experts who understand human behavior.

It's our duty to push new initiatives to our legislative representatives. This needs to be on a national level so proper funding can be made available at all levels of government. As the forensic sciences move ahead with standardized testing and reporting at a federal level, we must also strive to implement standardized procedures which address all aspects of these investigations.

Many jurisdictions conduct investigative grand juries on a regular basis; however, there are prohibitions in place to prevent those proceedings where the accused is deceased. It is hopeful that someday Molly's case, as well as all the others, are closed with a suspect being held responsible. Hopefully, that is not a pipedream. Through this collaborative effort, we as a society can at least do our part to minimize adding more unresolved homicides to the unacceptable number that has already been established.

JOHN W. DRAWEC, ESQ.

The unexpected and the incredible belong in this world.
Only then is life whole.

CARL JUNG

ACKNOWLEDGMENT

Thank You

To my family, you are why I am here. You gave me safety when I had none, strength when I couldn't find any, gave your love, your everything, and still do. You never lost faith in me. You give me hope. I am eternally grateful. I love you all.

To all the families I consulted for in Massachusetts, I am sorry I could not do more. I hope this book will help to bring about the changes we need in our criminal justice system. I love you all, and I keep you all in my heart every moment of every day.

DR. SARAH L. STEIN

ABOUT

SARAH L. STEIN, PH.D.

Dr. Sarah L. Stein is a consultant and co-founder for The Center for the Resolution of Unresolved Crime. Her areas of expertise include cold cases, victimology, suspectology, behavioral analysis, crime scene analysis, missing persons, interviews and interrogations, the social phenomenon of missing white woman syndrome, and how the influence of politics can affect progress and outcomes of unresolved cases.

Stein was awarded a Ph.D. in Criminal Justice in 2012, with a dissertation titled, "The Cultural Complex of Innocence: An Examination of the Social and Media Construction of Missing White Woman Syndrome."

She received a master's in Forensic Science with a concentration in Advanced Investigation and certification in Computer Forensics in

2007. Stein earned her bachelor's degree in 2004, from American University in Washington, D.C., with a self-designed major entitled "The Victimology of Pedophilia."

Stein has authored two chapters on cold cases, and published several articles related to the topic. Recent literary contributions include the chapter, Politics of Murder & the Challenges of Cold Cases, in the book, "Survivors: Shocking True Stories About America's Pursuit of Police Transparency & Justice" (2019), compiled by Dennis N. Griffin of The Transparency Project, and the chapter, Criminals: The Shadow Bearers of Society, in "Map of the Soul: Shadow, Our Hidden Self" (Stein, Buser, Cruz, & Stein, 2020).

"Who Took Molly Bish?" is the first in Stein's true crime series, When Criminal Justice Fails.

Stain now consults and teaches regularly for law enforcement agencies, and provides guidance for families both nationally and internationally.

CONTACT: info@drsarahstein.com
WEBSITE: www.Dr.SarahStein.com
CRUC: www.TheCruc.Com

OTHER ALYBLUE MEDIA TITLES

[PARTIAL LIST]

Survivors
Hidden Truths
A Child is Missing: A True Story
A Child is Missing: Searching for Justice
Color My Soul Whole
My Grief Diary
Grammy Visits From Heaven
Grandpa Visits From Heaven
Faith, Grief & Pass the Chocolate Pudding
Heaven Talks to Children
Crimson Sunshine
Grief Reiki
She, He, & Finding Me
Grief Diaries: Project Cold Case
Grief Diaries: Surviving Loss by Homicide
Grief Diaries: Surviving Sudden Loss
Grief Diaries: Surviving Loss by Cancer
Grief Diaries: Surviving Loss of a Spouse
Grief Diaries: Surviving Loss of a Child
Grief Diaries: Surviving Loss of a Sibling
Grief Diaries: Surviving Loss of a Parent
Grief Diaries: Surviving Loss of an Infant
Grief Diaries: Surviving Loss of a Loved One
Grief Diaries: Surviving Loss by Suicide
Grief Diaries: Surviving Loss of Health
Grief Diaries: How to Help the Newly Bereaved
Grief Diaries: Loss by Impaired Driving
Grief Diaries: Loss of a Pregnancy
Grief Diaries: Hello from Heaven
Grief Diaries: Grieving for the Living
Grief Diaries: Shattered
Grief Diaries: Through the Eyes of Men
Grief Diaries: Will We Survive?
Grief Diaries: Victim Impact Statement
Grief Diaries: Hit by Impaired Driver
Grief Diaries: Surviving Loss of a Pet
Real Life Diaries: Living with a Brain Injury
Real Life Diaries: Through the Eyes of DID
Real Life Diaries: Through the Eyes of an Eating Disorder
Real Life Diaries: Living with Endometriosis
Real Life Diaries: Living with Mental Illness

195

Humanity's legacy of stories and storytelling
is the most precious we have.

DORIS LESSING

*

PUBLISHED BY ALYBLUE MEDIA
Real stories. Real people. Real inspiration.
www.AlyBlueMedia.com

ENDNOTES

[1] https://www.mass.gov/service-details/victim-bill-of-rights

[2] www.ire.org

[3] https://www.ire.org/archives/30193

[4] https://theworldlink.com/news/local/mother-of-murdered-girl-settles-her-lawsuit/article_4d148bdf-5d4e-531f-b1d5-e6411bcc2945.html

[5] www.K9sardog.com

[6] https://www.capecodtimes.com/news/20190714/cape-woman-eyes-new-measures-to-identify-sisters-killer

[7] https://turtleboysports.com/da-joe-early-major-susan-anderson-force-troopers-to-alter-report-for-judges-daughter-who-said-do-you-know-how-many-people-i-had-to-blow-to-get-that-after-heroin-oui-arrest/

[8] https://www.telegram.com/news/20191101/da-joseph-early-and-state-police-pay-40k-in-settlement-with-trooper-who-arrested-judges-daughter

[9] https://www.telegram.com/news/20191101/da-joseph-early-and-state-police-pay-40k-in-settlement-with-trooper-who-arrested-judges-daughter

[10] https://en.wikipedia.org/wiki/Holly_Piirainen#Connection_to_Molly_Bish_case

[11] https://www.tapatalk.com/groups/thecyberseekerssociety/molly-bish-identified-t781-s20.html

[12] https://www.cnn.com/2010/CRIME/10/14/easy.prey.green.river.survivor/index.html

[13] https://enacademic.com/dic.nsf/enwiki/1889055

[14] https://www.telegram.com/article/20090128/NEWS/901280281

[15] http://transcripts.cnn.com/TRANSCRIPTS/0601/02/ng.01.html

[16] https://www.masslive.com/news/2007/06/john_bish_father_of_slain_life.html

[17] https://www.sentinelandenterprise.com/2007/10/11/fundraiser-to-benefit-bish-family-in-wake-of-fathers-recent-stroke/

[18] https://www.cnn.com/CNN/Programs/anderson.cooper.360/blog/2006/03/diagnosing-missing-white-woman.html

[19] Stein, 2012

[20] https://www.boston25news.com/news/molly-bish-rodney-stanger-may-have-crossed-paths-1/141310989/

[21] https://www.youtube.com/watch?v=aGAxHloQQ9c

[22] https://www.telegram.com/article/20141008/NEWS/310089852?template=ampart

[23] https://www.telegram.com/article/20080519/news/805190530

[24] https://www.boston25news.com/news/third-person-connected-to-bish-investigation-dies/138363727/

[25] https://www.milforddailynews.com/x2130789179

[26] https://obits.masslive.com/obituaries/masslive/obituary.aspx?n=john-borowiec&pid=155453358

[27] http://www.ncdsv.org/images/OJJDP_WhatAboutMe_5-2007.pdf

[28] https://www.telegram.com/article/20151005/NEWS/151009471

[29] Keppel, Robert & Walter, Richard. (1999). Profiling Killers: A Revised Classification Model for Understanding Sexual Murder. International Journal of Offender Therapy and Comparative Criminology - INT J OFFEND THER COMP CRIMIN. 43. 417-437.

[30] https://www.boston25news.com/news/have-you-seen-andy-puglisi-a-new-push-for-answers-40-years-later/427441027/

[31] https://www.cbsnews.com/news/part-ii-the-mystery-man-16-08-2004/

[32] https://turtleboysports.com/just-like-we-said-government-officials-claim-da-joe-early-communicated-directly-with-colonel-mckeon-to-redact-alli-bibauds-arrest-report/

[33] https://www.telegram.com/news/20200102/worcester-lawyer-blake-rubin-one-time-da-candidate-faces-witness-intimidation-and-conspiracy-charges

[34] https://www.bostonglobe.com/metro/2019/11/06/state-police-boss-col-kerry-gilpin-steps-down-annouces-retirement/IguHlxVZkmug7iuxZ1nmK/story.html

[35] https://www.masslive.com/news/2018/05/michael_hand_indicted_for_murd.html

[36] https://nccs.net/blogs/americas-founding-documents/bill-of-rights-amendments-1-10

[37] https://www.nbc12.com/2020/05/27/body-year-old-boy-who-went-missing-memorial-day-found-calif-river/?outputType=amp

[38] https://www.salary.com/research/salary/alternate/police-officer-salary

[39] https://en.wikipedia.org/wiki/Murder_of_Bella_Bond

[40] https://www.murderdata.org

[41] https://www.southcoasttoday.com/apps/pbcs.dll/article?AID=/20120826/NEWS21/208260351/-1/NEWS01

[42] https://www.masslive.com/news/2016/09/cold_case_homicides_in_massach.html

[43] https://www.wcvb.com/article/dna-test-results-breed-cautious-optimism-in-molly-bish-murder-investigation/10237140

[44] https://www.capecodtimes.com/news/20190714/cape-woman-eyes-new-measures-to-identify-sisters-killer

[45] https://www.capecodtimes.com/news/20190714/cape-woman-eyes-new-measures-to-identify-sisters-killer

[46] https://www.wcvb.com/article/dna-test-results-breed-cautious-optimism-in-molly-bish-murder-investigation/10237140

[47] https://www.goodreads.com/quotes/11414-truth-never-damages-a-cause-that-is-just